ANUNNAKI REVELATION

Other New Page Books by Heather Lynn

The Anunnaki Connection (2020)
Baphomet Revealed (2024)
Evil Archaeology (2019)

ANUNNAKI REVELATION

Hidden History, Altered States, *and the* Mystery *of* Humanity

HEATHER LYNN, PHD

This edition first published in 2026 by New Page Books, an imprint of

Red Wheel/Weiser, LLC
With offices at:
65 Parker Street, Suite 7
Newburyport, MA 01950
www.redwheelweiser.com

ISBN: 978-1-63748-022-9
Library of Congress Cataloging-in-Publication Data available upon request.

Cover design by Sky Peck Design
Cover collage by Sky Peck Design
Images on pages 7, 98, 100, 102, 108, 182, 190, 192, 208, WikiCommons
Images on pages 3, 10, 11, ShareAlike 4.0 International (CC BY_SA 4.0)
Image on page 86, Heather Lynn
Image on page 90, Adobe Stock
Image on pages 96, Alamy
Interior by Happenstance Type-O-Rama
Typeset in Change, Cormorant Garamond, and NEWLOOK

Printed in the United States
IBI
10 9 8 7 6 5 4 3 2 1

This book is dedicated to

The Academics, *who dare not tread down adventurous paths for fear of losing what took so long to achieve. I may have chosen a different path, but I understand why you stay.*

The Intrepid Armchair Researchers, *who are brave enough to follow their curiosity to some wild places and honest enough to follow the research wherever it leads. Let's goooo!!!*

The Stoners and Psychonauts, *who glimpsed truths through altered states but whose insights were dismissed because they didn't fit the mold. You saw something real, something profound, long before the rest of us. May your third eye stay wide open! The playa provides!*

The Curious Minds, *who may not have walked the halls of academia but who possess keen minds and an unyielding quest for truth. Your wisdom stems from a life lived and not lectures. The world is your classroom!*

The Prideful Skeptics, *who pride themselves on doubting everything. Remember, Einstein read mystics to mine ideas, Newton studied alchemy, and Tesla attributed his inventions to vivid dreams and visions. Your scrutiny is valuable, but don't let it blind you to the intuitive flashes that have often sparked scientific breakthroughs.*

The Lost, *who are drawn to charismatic figures promising cosmic secrets. You cannot be empowered by giving your power to others, as true empowerment comes from within. Question everything, trust your instincts, and know we're all seekers on this path together. Stay strong!*

CONTENTS

ACKNOWLEDGMENTS

I would like to thank Michael Pye, Eryn Eaton, and everyone at Red Wheel/Weiser for their unwavering support and belief in this project. Thank you to members of The Midnight Academy, especially James Williams, B. T. Wallace, Crypto Kev, and Israel Sanchez. Thank you for being friends and colleagues in the pursuit of truth.

INTRODUCTION
A Journey into the Light

We are part of a symbiotic relationship with
something which disguises itself as an
extra-terrestrial invasion so as not to alarm us.

—TERENCE MCKENNA, *The Archaic Revival*

With closed eyes, I focused my attention on the so-called third eye in the middle of my forehead, as I was instructed. After a few minutes, I was engulfed by a kaleidoscope of colors and lights. As I continued to focus, the colors swirled and became more vivid, turning from red to blue to indigo. I got caught up in observing the beauty of this light and how it behaved independent of my direct will. Soon, the colors morphed together, blending into a warm, golden orb that seemed to be growing. It was like a golden flame, with a warm glow and flicker, but still fluid in form. I was transfixed, no longer distracted internally or externally, because this light show was fascinating. As the warm, golden flame grew in size, it also became brighter.

As the light grew, I suddenly felt an odd sense of happiness for no apparent reason. The brighter the light became, the more elated I felt, until it seemed to flash into a bright white so intense that I squeezed my eyes closed as hard as I could. My brain thought I needed to do this, but the light was not external; it was coming from within. It felt like the light was pouring over me with warmth, like being bathed in sunlight, and with this warmth came a strange sense of being loved. I was ecstatic, feeling love I had never experienced before. A tear rolled down my face, but even acknowledging that physical sensation didn't disconnect me from the moment. I felt nothing but the warm embrace of love and light.

I know how "woo-woo" this sounds, but suddenly, that feeling of love became embodied. It felt like someone was right there with me. I kept gazing into the light when it started to move again, this time looking like an image trying to render from some AI program. But the warmth soon gave way to an ominous sense of threat. The form quickly took on a more geometric nature, and out from the center emerged a strange, angular face that I can only describe as a cross between an elf and a reptile; it was comprised of a grid-like pattern, resembling a machine-like version of an Ubaid Lizardmen statue, with an elongated head, almond-shaped eyes, and a lizard-like snout—some have interpreted such statues as depicting a reptilian humanoid figures.

I sensed the entity speak; I didn't hear it, but felt it. It began saying, "Come and see . . . ," but before it could go on, I reached a moment of lucidity and forced my eyes open. Standing up, I thought, "NO! I am *not* doing this." I knew then that I couldn't continue this practice. It had become too real, throwing me into an existential crisis. What did I see? How could meditating cause me to hallucinate? Was it a hallucination, or was it real? And what is "real," anyway?

I stepped back from the practice of theurgy through meditation and decided not to speak of it. After all, I want to *know*, not believe. Nevertheless, the experience haunted me, and as I

Lizard-headed figure from Ur, Iraq, c. 4000 BCE

continued my research on ancient civilizations and their mythologies, I couldn't shake the feeling that there was a connection between the entity I encountered and the stories of the Anunnaki, the powerful deities of the ancient Mesopotamian pantheon.

I don't have experiences, in the supernatural sense, nor am I an empath, lightworker, or any of the other buzzwords I've heard thrown around in New Age circles. I would consider myself a bit mundane—dare I say skeptical? So when I came face to face with what appeared to be a geometric self-creating entity during an arcane meditation practice, I was forced to question everything I thought I knew about reality, consciousness, and the nature of existence itself.

Growing up, I attended a Catholic school where we had weekly contemplative prayer sessions, a form of Jesuit meditation. While my classmates fidgeted and whispered, I sat quietly in the church pew, hoping to hear the voice of God. I longed to ask him big questions about my parents' divorce, the troubles at home, and even the mysteries of the universe. I wanted to know about things most important to a child, like dinosaurs, unicorns, and the existence of aliens. I yearned for God to be the anthropomorphic father figure who could fix my life and give me the truth about things we may never know. No matter how hard I tried, though, I could not seem to quiet my mind enough to experience the divine connection I craved.

This struggle with meditation followed me into adulthood. Despite exploring various practices, from Buddhist meditation in the Mojave Desert to the mystery teachings of an occult organization, I believed that I simply wasn't one of those experiencers who could achieve profound states of spiritual enlightenment. That remained the case until a fateful encounter during a full moon meditation, part of an occult mystery school practice, forced me to confront the reality of altered states of consciousness and the potential existence of what I and the scientific literature call *discarnate entities*, or entities with no physical bodies.

The Question

The more I studied these entities, the more parallels to the sages of ancient civilization I started to discover, and the more I realized that my experience was not unique. In many past cultures, people reported encounters with otherworldly beings during altered states of consciousness, whether induced by meditation, shamanic practices, or the use of psychedelics. These experiences have often been linked to the acquisition of hidden knowledge and the transformation of human consciousness. As I explored the ancient texts and artifacts of Mesopotamia, I began to see striking parallels between the entity I encountered and the figures described in the earliest mythological records. The Anunnaki appear in Sumerian, Akkadian, and Babylonian traditions as powerful divine beings who descended from the heavens and played a central role in shaping the foundations of human civilization. They were said to have established kingship, delineated social order, and transmitted knowledge to humanity. This transmission was not limited to practical or technical instruction but often carried symbolic, cosmological, or even initiatory weight. In some depictions, they bore anthropomorphic features alongside serpentine or reptilian elements, suggesting a hybrid nature that was neither fully divine nor fully terrestrial.

Could it be that the Anunnaki were not merely mythological constructs but actual discarnate entities that communicated with humans through altered states of consciousness? What I discovered in the years that followed was both thrilling and disquieting, taking me to places—both literal and metaphorical—that I never expected to go. This book is as much about that journey as it is about the mysteries of the Anunnaki.

It may at first seem like a giant leap, but whether the Anunnaki were discarnate entities was a question that became the driving force behind my research, leading me to investigate the role of psychedelics, shamanic practices, and meditation in accessing other realms of reality and communicating with otherworldly beings. This quest took me down a path where I began to uncover a complex web of connections between the Anunnaki, occult magic, secret societies, human consciousness, and the evolution of our species. This book is my attempt to unveil the secrets of the Anunnaki and their enduring influence on human origin and history. From the mysterious building techniques of the ancient world to the cutting-edge research of modern science and the frontiers of artificial intelligence, we will explore the ways in which these entities have molded us "in their image" and why.

The Sumerian Mushroom Tablets

In John Allegro's provocative book, *The Sacred Mushroom and the Cross* (1970) he posited that early Christianity was a mushroom cult and that the Bible contained coded references to psychedelic experiences. Allegro's ideas were met with widespread criticism and dismissal from the academic community, but they struck a chord with many in the psychedelic underground who saw them as validation of their own experiences. Allegro argued that the use of sacred mushrooms, particularly the species *Amanita muscaria*, was central to the religious practices of the ancient world and that these mushrooms were seen as a means of communicating with the divine. He draws parallels between the biblical accounts of prophetic visions and the experiences reported by those who had consumed sacred mushrooms. He suggests that the "burning bush" encountered by Moses, the "tongues of fire" that descended on the apostles at Pentecost, and the visions of the Book of Revelation all bear the hallmarks of psychedelic experiences.

While Allegro's ideas remain controversial and are not widely accepted by mainstream scholars, they do raise intriguing questions about the role of psychedelics in the history of religion and spirituality. If, as Allegro suggests, the use of sacred mushrooms and other psychedelic plants was more widespread in the ancient world than previously thought, then it is possible that many of the foundational religious and spiritual experiences that shaped human culture were influenced by these substances.

In the ruins of ancient Uruk, archaeologists uncovered a collection of mushroom-shaped clay objects concealed within temple walls. These artifacts, known as the Tonpilze, were inscribed in Sumerian cuneiform with invocations from King Sîn-kāšid to the gods Lugal-irra and Meslamta-ea. Unlike typical public inscriptions, these tablets were hidden from view, never meant for human eyes. Their placement suggests they were not written for the living but for the gods themselves, forming a kind of sealed transmission between king and deity. These mushrooms have been compared to *sikkatu pegs*, as detailed in the study of Old Babylonian legal texts.

Mushrooms with cuneiform inscriptions of Gudea, ruler of Lagash, c. 2144–2124 BCE

According to Lotte Oers in her analysis of the sikkatu in Old Babylonian Susa, these pegs were driven into property to mark ownership or pledge a property as collateral in transactions involving loans or leases. The act of driving the sikkatu was recorded in legal contracts, thus intertwining the spiritual act of securing divine protection with the bureaucratic need for legal documentation (Oers, 2010). The clay mushrooms found at Uruk, however, represent a more overtly spiritual use of symbolic objects. These mushrooms, inscribed with dedications by King Sîn-kāšid, were offerings meant to secure the favor of the gods and ensure the king's legacy as a just and righteous ruler (Sieckmeyer, 2024).

The evolution from the hidden, god-focused mushrooms to the more bureaucratically integrated sikkatu reflects broader changes in Mesopotamian society as it transitioned from the Sumerian to the Akkadian period. The Akkadians, while inheriting the spiritual traditions of their predecessors, adapted these practices into a more structured, bureaucratic framework that reflected the needs of their growing empire. This blend of spirituality and bureaucracy underscores the complex relationship between the divine and the state in ancient Mesopotamia, where legal and spiritual authority were often one and the same. The discovery of these mushroom tablets raises more questions about the Sumerians' relationship with their deities and the role of psychoactive substances in their religious practices. Could the deliberate shaping of the tablets into mushroom forms and their placement within sacred temple walls suggest that the Sumerians saw mushrooms as the conduit of communication between gods and man?

The Ultraterrestrial Hypothesis

The traditional view of the Anunnaki as gods, or, in more recent popular theories, as ancient astronauts, has shaped the way we interpret Mesopotamian mythology for over a century. Yet both frameworks may be too narrow. The evidence suggests we are not dealing with biological beings from another planet, nor simply symbolic projections of the human psyche. What emerges instead is a third possibility: the Anunnaki as *ultraterrestrials*. These entities, if they existed, would not travel in spacecraft but operate through consciousness, energy, and form. They would be native to Earth's metaphysical landscape, revealing themselves only in states of altered perception or through encoded rituals, such as the ones hinted at in the mushroom tablets of Uruk. This interpretation opens new questions, not just about who the Anunnaki were, but about the very nature of contact, consciousness, and civilization itself. This is the lens I will use throughout this book: The Anunnaki may not have been myths or astronauts, but rather ultraterrestrial intelligences that move through human consciousness, our civilizations, and perhaps even our future technologies.

The Anunnaki have been the subject of countless myths, legends, and speculative theories, all of which revolve around the idea of powerful, otherworldly beings who have played a key role in shaping human history and consciousness. Whether the gods of Mesopotamia were actual deities or merely mythological constructs, their enduring influence on human culture and consciousness is valid, but still highly controversial.

The history of human knowledge is filled with examples of radical ideas that were initially dismissed or ridiculed, only to be vindicated by later discoveries and insights. The discovery that the Sumerian deities may have communicated with humans through psychedelic experiences and altered states of consciousness raises profound questions about the nature of reality, the origins of human civilization, and the potential for contact with otherworldly beings.

However, these ideas are not merely academic or theoretical concerns. They have practical implications for how we approach the challenges and opportunities of the twenty-first century and beyond, with one of the most pressing challenges facing humanity today being the rapid development of artificial intelligence and other advanced technologies. As we continue to push the boundaries of what is possible with these technologies, we are confronted with fundamental questions about the nature of consciousness, the boundaries between the natural and the artificial, and the potential for the creating new forms of intelligence and sentience.

Could the Anunnaki's apparent mastery of advanced technology and their ability to manipulate matter and energy hold clues for how we might approach these challenges? In the chapters ahead, we will begin to explore the profound influence that the Anunnaki and other similar beings have had on human history, consciousness, and the quest for hidden knowledge. Together, we will cover these questions:

- Who were the Anunnaki? Were they benevolent guides or malevolent manipulators, and what will the answer mean for our understanding of the nature of reality?
- Was the Anunnaki's wisdom transmitted to early civilization, then preserved and passed down through secret societies and occult practices?
- Were psychedelics, shamanic practices, and altered states of consciousness used to communicate with the Anunnaki and other entities? Are they still?
- Did the Anunnaki influence the development of ancient technology?
- How could the Anunnaki's claims of mastery over death inform our approach to artificial intelligence, longevity, and the transhumanist quest for immortality?

We will also dig into the mysteries of the Anunnaki and their enduring influence on human consciousness and culture. Those familiar with my work know that I refrain from making absolute claims about the past. Instead, I engage in questioning historiography, analyzing material evidence, and presenting various perspectives. Moreover, I am not a fan of those overhyping or glamorizing research in this field as it often leads to the formation of cults of personality. When individuals become captivated by a particular researcher's fame, they may cease to question and explore further, leading to a stagnation of intellectual inquiry. This fixation can prevent the progression of new ideas and deeper understanding no matter what field.

However, during my research for this book, I uncovered compelling archaeological and historical evidence suggesting that the Sumerians used mind-altering substances to commune with the Apkallu and initiate their kings into what I propose was the Cult of the Poppy. It is centered around a ritual I refer to as the *Hul Gil Rite* (*Hul Gil*, means "joy plant," in Sumerian). I understand that the conclusions I present here will be controversial, potentially placing me at odds with both mainstream scholars and fringe theorists. Yet, I trust that my readers, who have come to value my dedication to uncovering the truth about our ancient past, will approach this evidence with open minds. I aim to offer fresh perspectives on the Anunnaki that challenge both established narratives and fringe theories alike. I question those who view the Anunnaki as mere mythological beings and confront the notion of them as space-faring visitors with technology reminiscent of mid-twentieth century NASA. Moreover, I critically examine the emerging New Age narratives that blend alien theories with law of attraction and prosperity gospels, creating a kind of global extraterrestrial religion. I do not seek to convince you of anything but rather to present an open and honest inquiry for your consideration.

Since writing *The Anunnaki Connection*, I've grappled with deeper questions about who the Anunnaki are and where they might be now. Years of relentless research forced me to reevaluate everything I thought I knew; my faith; and my understanding of history, society, and the very nature of reality. This journey led me far beyond the sterile confines of academia into hidden, dust-shrouded archives and the shadowed circles of clandestine occultists. I found myself among *psychonauts*, explorers of inner space whose altered states of consciousness are expanded by substances known to shamans and mystics for millennia.

This book is not simply a chronicle of archaeological discovery, but a *revelation* of occulted knowledge—a journey that has challenged the very fabric of our history and the origins of humanity itself. Within these pages, you will be invited to explore mysteries that bridge the physical and the spiritual, the historical and the mythical. The book invites you to join me in a quest that spans not only time and space but the boundaries of human consciousness. What you are about to read may well reshape your perception of our past, our present, and the hidden forces that have shaped our world.

I invite you to consider the possibility that the story of the Anunnaki may be more than just a myth or a legend. It may be a key to unlocking the secrets of our past and the potential of our future, a doorway to a new understanding of who (or what) we *really* are. Come and see . . .

CHAPTER 1

THE RIDDLE OF THE ANUNNAKI

From Stardust to Civilization

We are all stardust, and the magic of the universe is within us all.

—CARL SAGAN

The early twentieth century marked a significant turning point in our understanding of ancient civilizations, particularly with the discovery of cuneiform tablets in Mesopotamia. These ancient texts, such as the *Enuma Elish* and the *Epic of Gilgamesh*, not only provided profound insights into the societal structures and beliefs of early Sumerians but also introduced the world to the entities known as the Anunnaki. To begin to understand the Anunnaki, we must first understand the Sumerian people.

In the fertile lands between the Tigris and Euphrates rivers, where the soil was rich and the waters life-giving, a remarkable civilization emerged that would forever change the course of human history. This land, known to the ancient Greeks as Mesopotamia—"the land between the rivers"—witnessed the birth of the world's first great cities and the rise of a people whose innovations would shape the foundations of human society for millennia to come. These people were the Sumerians, and their story is one of ingenuity, ambition, and the relentless pursuit of knowledge and power.

As the fourth millennium BCE drew to a close, the landscape of southern Mesopotamia was undergoing a profound transformation. What had once been a scattering of small farming villages was rapidly evolving into a network of bustling urban centers. By around 3000 BCE, the region we now call Sumer was home to an impressive array of settlements: one hundred twenty-four villages with populations of about one hundred residents each, twenty towns boasting up to two thousand inhabitants, another twenty small urban centers with as many as five thousand people, and at the heart of it all, the great city of Uruk, whose population may have swelled to an astonishing fifty thousand souls.

This explosive urban growth was more than just a demographic shift; it was the crucible in which the very concept of civilization as we know it was forged. The challenges and opportunities presented by life in these densely populated centers spurred the Sumerians to new heights of innovation and social organization. The need to manage resources, coordinate labor, and maintain order in these burgeoning cities led to the development of complex political structures, sophisticated economic systems, and intricate social hierarchies.

The Sumerians were not content merely to build cities; they sought to reshape their world through technological innovation. The fourth millennium BCE saw a flurry of inventions that would transform every aspect of Sumerian life and leave an indelible mark on human history. One of the most significant breakthroughs came with the advent of bronze manufacturing. This alloy of tin and copper, harder and more durable than either of its component metals, ushered in the Bronze Age in Mesopotamia. For nearly three thousand years, bronze would reign supreme as the material of choice for tools and weapons, enabling unprecedented advances in agriculture, construction, and warfare.

Yet among all the Sumerians' remarkable achievements, one stands out as perhaps their greatest gift to humanity: the invention of writing. Around 3000 BCE, the Sumerians developed cuneiform, a script characterized by wedge-shaped symbols pressed into clay tablets. This revolutionary system of communication began as a means of recording commercial transactions, contracts, and administrative details. However, it quickly evolved into a versatile tool for preserving knowledge, codifying laws, and giving voice to the Sumerian culture.

The impact of cuneiform on human civilization cannot be overstated. It allowed knowledge to be accumulated and transmitted across generations, facilitating the growth of complex societies and the preservation of cultural heritage. The clay tablets on which cuneiform was inscribed proved remarkably durable, providing modern scholars with an unparalleled window into the daily lives, beliefs, and aspirations of the ancient Sumerians.

The development of writing was not merely a technological innovation; it was a cognitive revolution. The ability to render language in symbolic form opened up new realms of abstract thought and creative expression. It enabled the Sumerians to craft elaborate mythologies, compose stirring poetry, and record the deeds of kings and gods for posterity. The *Epic of Gilgamesh*, one of the earliest known works of literature, stands as a testament to the power of the written word to capture the human experience and explore the deepest questions of existence.

The Sumerians inhabited a world alive with divine presence. Their polytheistic religion recognized a vast pantheon of gods, each associated with different aspects of the natural world and human experience. At the heart of Sumerian religious life was the belief that these deities were intimately involved in the affairs of mortals, capable of bestowing blessings or unleashing devastation according to their whims. These deities, however, were far from being perfect or wholly benevolent. Instead they exhibited a wide range of human-like behaviors and flaws. The religious texts of the Sumerians, Akkadians, and Babylonians paint a picture of gods engaged in acts of creation and destruction, displaying traits such as intoxication, sexual promiscuity, wrath, jealousy, selfishness, and arrogance. These characteristics manifested in their interactions with each other, as well as in their dealings with humans and demigods. Ancient religion served multiple purposes, but it is a mistake to look at it through a modern lens and assume that people looked to their gods as examples of a moral life. Back then, people would not have worn bracelets with the letters WWZD, asking "what would Zeus do?" These gods were understood in a wholly different way.

However, it would also be a mistake to interpret these traits as indicative of purely immoral or malevolent deities. The same pantheon that showcased such flaws also included gods who acted as benevolent protectors and teachers of humanity. Many narratives depict these divine beings assisting mortals, curing illnesses, and preserving lives. Unlike later monotheistic traditions, Mesopotamian gods were not seen as inherently just or good. Instead, they could be capricious, vindictive, or even unjust from a human perspective. This led to complex theological discussions about the nature of suffering, the role of personal piety, and the limits of human understanding of divine will. Texts like the "Babylonian Theodicy" and the dialogue between a man and his god grapple with these issues, demonstrating a sophisticated approach to questions of theodicy (Oshima, 2014).

The gods were more than just personifications of natural phenomena or abstract concepts. They were often portrayed as cosmic engineers, actively shaping the world and civilization through both ideological influence and physical intervention. This portrayal of the gods as hands-on shapers of reality sets Mesopotamian mythology apart from some other ancient belief systems where gods were seen as more distant or abstract entities. In many cases, the gods took on the role of instructors, imparting knowledge and skills to humanity. Before we go further, let's try to set a clear outline of what the Mesopotamians believed about their gods.

Understanding the Mesopotamian Pantheon

Mesopotamian religion was around for a long time and was practiced by many different cultures across hundreds of miles and thousands of years. Each culture had its own slightly different take on how they practiced religion, so there are no definitive versions of these stories. There can be quite a bit of overlap between the duties of different gods, and which gods are most important can vary. When the Sumerians first adopted the religion, different cities had different patron deities. As certain cities like Akkad, Assur, or Babylon built their empires, their patron deity became more important and often adopted the qualities of gods that used to be more important in different cities.

In short, there is no Mesopotamian bible to give us a single definitive canon and the Mesopotamian creation myths evolved over time and across different cultures, leading to multiple versions and variations. Understanding these can be challenging due to the overlapping roles and differing genealogies. The following is a clarification of some key points.

The Source

Nammu is often considered the primordial source in early Sumerian mythology. She is the goddess of the primeval sea and is said to have given birth to An (the sky; also known as Anu) and Ki (the earth). Nammu is also the mother of Enki (god of wisdom and water), also known as Ea. In some versions, Nammu plays a central role in creation by giving birth to the first gods, including Enki. In later Babylonian mythology, particularly in the *Enuma Elish*, Anshar (sky axis) and Kishar (earth axis) are depicted as primordial forces. They are the parents of An (also known as Urash, and later Antu). This version introduces a different genealogy where Anshar and Kishar are seen as ancestors of the gods, including An. In the Babylonian creation epic *Enuma Elish*, Abzu (freshwater) and Tiamat (saltwater) are primordial beings. From their union, the younger gods are born, eventually leading to the rise of Marduk after he defeats Tiamat.

The differences in these myths often reflect how the stories evolved over time and across various Mesopotamian cultures. The Sumerians had one set of creation stories, while the Babylonians adapted these myths to fit their own religious beliefs. As different Mesopotamian cultures interacted, their myths often merged, resulting in multiple, sometimes contradictory versions of the same stories. Further, different city-states had their own local traditions, leading to variations in the details of divine genealogy. For example, while Enlil was the chief god in Nippur, Marduk became the chief god in Babylon.

In some Sumerian traditions, Nammu is depicted as giving birth to An and Ki. She is also considered the mother of Enki and Enlil in certain myths. In a more widely recognized version, An and Ki are a pair, and their union produces the younger gods, including Enlil. It is important to remember that Ki and Nammu are distinct figures. Ki is the earth goddess and consort of An. Nammu is the primordial sea goddess, the mother of Enki, and sometimes she is regarded as the creator of heaven and earth. While their roles may overlap in some traditions, they are generally considered separate deities.

Heaven, Earth, and the Bloodline of the Gods

Anshar and Kishar are the first instance, both within this family tree and historically, of a very popular trope among many polytheistic religions: that of the sky father and earth mother. Their children, An and Ki, fulfill the same role as their parents. An was the supreme god but was rarely worshipped and sort of fell into the background. His most important role in society was being the god of divinity itself. He transferred divine authority to kings on earth and gods alike. Ki, the Sumerian earth goddess, was also referred to as Urash, a name associated with agricultural abundance and feminine generativity. She was later supplanted by Antu in Akkadian cosmology. It was believed that the rain was An's seed, and when the rain came down, the earth became pregnant, and Ki thereby gave birth to all things. Alongside the plants, Ki gave birth to the Anunnaki, who are similar to the Olympians of Greek mythology or the Aesir of Norse mythology and were believed to hold the fates of humans in their hands. The two most important of the Anunnaki were the brothers Enlil and Enki.

Enlil, in contrast to his father An, was worshipped extensively. He was seen as the ultimate benevolent father figure and was so holy that even certain other gods couldn't look upon him. Enlil was responsible for the creation of civilization, and his temple was the anchor between heaven and earth. His wife was Ninlil, who was the lady of the wind or lady of the open field. When they met, Enlil seduced Ninlil by the riverside, and they conceived Nanna, god of the moon. Enlil was then sent to the underworld for his ritually impure relationship with Ninlil, but she followed him. Along the way, she encounters Enlil three more times, disguised as the gatekeeper of the city he'd left, the river of the underworld, and the underworld's ferryman. Each time, Ninlil is seduced and impregnated with a new deity: a god of canals, a god with a curious dual association with both the underworld and healing, and most importantly, the god of death, Nergal.

Enlil is also important in the Mesopotamian flood myth, another point of similarity with later religions. Originally, the story went that there was a great flood, and Enlil rewarded the sole survivor, Utnapishtim, with immortality. But in later tellings, Enlil was the cause of the flood. Enlil couldn't sleep because too many humans on the earth were making noise, so he decided to kill every living thing with a flood. His brother Enki warned Utnapishtim of the oncoming flood, so he and his family became the only survivors. Enlil had several children, each with different domains and temperaments. Among them were Ninurta, a warrior god associated with agriculture and justice, and Nanna, the moon god, whose daughter Inanna would become one of the most powerful and complex deities in the entire Mesopotamian pantheon. Enlil was furious to see humans still walking the earth, but his son Ninurta and his granddaughter Inanna convinced him to promise never to flood the earth again, and instead to periodically cull the human population with wild animals and famines.

Enki is a god of creation as well as a trickster figure. At times heroic, at times villainous, and at others just plain lazy, he's a central figure in the creation of humanity. In one story, Abzu was growing old and tired, but he was disturbed by the ruckus of the younger gods. So he set out to destroy them. The gods found out about this, and Enki stepped forward as their point guard. He placed Abzu in a deep sleep and carried him deep underground. This begged the question: Who would care for Abzu's primordial waters while he slept? So Enki dove deep down to the freshwater sea beneath the earth to rule Abzu's realm in his stead.

Tiamat was not happy with their children usurping Abzu, so she transformed into a terrifying dragon to destroy the world herself. This time, Enki chose to do nothing. So Enlil stepped up to slay the dragon. He tore her body apart, making the vault of the heavens with her ribs and the Milky Way with her tail. But of course, she couldn't truly be killed, and so she carried on living in that disfigured form. From her crying eyes sprang forth the rivers Tigris and Euphrates.

Enki was also promiscuous and deceitful. In one sordid tale, Enki has an affair with Ninhursag, a fertility goddess, but eventually, she leaves him. Some years later, Enki is still lonely and missing his lost lover when a beautiful young woman who looks just like Ninhursag appears. Enki seduces her, unaware that the young woman is actually his daughter by Ninhursag. After she leaves him, time passes, and Enki finds himself once again alone and longing for connection. He meets another beautiful maiden, not realizing that she is both his daughter and his granddaughter. He seduces her as well. Eventually, a third young woman appears, bearing an uncanny resemblance to Ninhursag. She is his daughter, his granddaughter, and his great-granddaughter. If her DNA were analyzed, it would be 87.5 percent Enki. When Ninhursag discovers what has happened, she takes action. Enki's body begins to swell, each part afflicted with unbearable pain. Only after Ninhursag decides to show mercy does she relieve his suffering, removing the swelling organ by organ and creating from each one a new god of healing.

Other Important Deities

Aside from that ultimate incestuous line, Enki had a son named Marduk who became the patron god of Babylon. He used to be a very minor god until the reign of Hammurabi, during which Babylon conquered much of the Fertile Crescent. Marduk then took on the roles and myths of both Enki and Enlil. According to Babylonian tradition, it was Marduk who slayed Abzu and defeated Tiamat. He's also associated with the planet Jupiter and so is sometimes seen as the equivalent to the Roman Jupiter, though their similarities are limited.

Returning to Enlil and Ninlil's side of the family tree, their son Ninurta is associated with farming and healing, whether alleviating sickness or driving out demons. He's associated with the planet Saturn and the Roman Saturn (aka Cronus). Again, it's not an exact match, but they do share similar themes of farming and the passage of time. Eventually, Ninurta became associated with war as well.

Ninurta enjoyed much popularity during the Neo-Assyrian Empire, during a time when the empire was largely henotheistic, meaning they acknowledged the existence of many gods but only worshiped one, in this case usually the god Ashur, who was likely the Assyrian equivalent of Enlil. But after the fall of the empire, Ninurta became too closely associated with the oppressive, warlike regime, so his statues were torn down and he faded once again into obscurity. Though sometimes presented as the son of Ninlil, other stories claim he's the son of Ninhursag. That's because after defeating a mighty army with the help of his talking mace, he used his enemies' fallen stone soldiers to construct the mountains and the hills, dedicating them to his mother, whom he renamed Ninhursag, which means "lady of the mountain."

Ninurta is also known for defeating the Anzu, a giant bird that stole his father Enlil's Tablet of Destinies, the object that denoted his divine right to rule. Ninurta shot the bird with arrows, but the tablet had the ability to turn back time, so the arrow's shaft turned into a cane, the flint heads returned to the quarry, and the feathers turned into a bird. This is particularly interesting as most classical or medieval stories that depict any kind of time travel almost always refer to moving forward in time; most stories about going backward are much more recent. Ultimately, Ninurta summons a wind that rips the bird's wings off, and then he slits its throat.

Nanna, also known as Sin (not because he was evil, Sin just happens to be the name he took in the ancient Semitic polytheistic religion), is a little unique in that he is a male moon god rather than the more common moon goddess. He has a beard of lapis lazuli and rides a winged bull. Other than that, we don't know much about him because his time in the spotlight was when Ur was the most powerful of the Sumerian city-states, around 2600–2400 BCE. However, the famous ziggurat of Ur was dedicated to him, so he still has that distinction.

Then there is Nabu, son of Marduk and god of wisdom, writing, and prophecies. He was believed to inscribe the fates decreed by the gods and came to embody the power of the written word itself. Nabu was associated with the planet Mercury and was later identified with the Greco-Roman god Mercury due to their shared role as divine messengers and keepers of knowledge. Yet Nabu also bears some resemblance to Apollo, particularly in his role as a giver of oracles and one who reveals the will of the divine through inspired communication.

Inanna, the Sumerian goddess of love, beauty, and political power, is courted in one early myth by two suitors: Enkimdu, a farmer, and Dumuzi, a shepherd. At first she favors the farmer, but eventually she chooses the shepherd because he brings her better gifts and argues more persuasively. The structure of the story is reminiscent of the biblical account of Cain and Abel, in which a farmer and a shepherd make competing offerings. In both cases, the shepherd's offering is ultimately preferred, reflecting a cultural hierarchy that elevates pastoralism and divine favor over agriculture. Anyway, Inanna and Dumuzi live happily ever after until she decides to descend to the underworld and finds herself trapped there.

When Inanna finally escapes the underworld, the demons who followed her insist that someone must take her place, as no one can leave the land of the dead without a substitute. She looks for someone to sacrifice and finds Dumuzi seated on his throne, dressed in his finest clothes, showing no sign of mourning her absence. Outraged by his indifference, she hands him over to the demons. Later, moved by pity, Inanna negotiates an arrangement in which Dumuzi spends half the year in the underworld and half on the surface, a cycle understood to explain the changing of the seasons. This story likely influenced the later Greek myth of Persephone and Hades.

Next is Inanna's twin brother Utu. Because he is the god of justice, Utu tried to help Dumuzi when the demons came to drag him to the underworld. Utu's also the god of the sun; he rides a chariot across the sky during the day and travels through the underworld at night. His position from the sky allows him to see everything on the earth and therefore he can enforce justice, truth, and morality among mortals.

Here's a fun fact about Utu: There is actually a carved portrait of Utu in the US House Chamber, just above the gallery doors. In 1950, portraits of famous lawmakers and philosophers were added to the chamber, and this one, supposedly of Hammurabi, was based off of a figure in the Hammurabi stele who is sitting on his throne and wearing a spiraling hat. However, the man sitting on the throne isn't actually Hammurabi. In all of Hammurabi's depictions, he has a round hat that looks like a helmet, whereas Utu, who has a higher station than a king, is depicted on a throne wearing a spiraling hat.

Finally, let's talk about Ereshkigal and Nergal. Nergal is sometimes associated with Enlil in later traditions, and Ereshkigal is Inanna and Utu's older sister, though she's not really associated with them that often aside from her role in the story about Inanna's descent into the underworld. The primary myth having to do with her is about her marriage. One day, a banquet takes place that Ereshkigal can't attend because she's queen of the underworld, and the other gods don't want to throw a party there because people have a tendency to get trapped. So Ereshkigal sends someone to the banquet on her behalf. At the party, Nergal is rude to Ereshkigal's envoy, so she summons him to the underworld.

He's told that if he ever wants to make it out alive, he cannot eat, drink, wash, or sit in Ereshkigal's kingdom. He also is told that he can't sleep with the goddess of the underworld, and that turns out to be more of a challenge for him. He tries to leave after having an affair with Ereshkigal, but she drags him back down even after he tries to disguise himself. Despite initially being called down to the underworld as punishment, Nergal becomes king of the underworld when the two get married. This duality of Ereshkigal and Nergal, with love and death intertwined, strikes me as a mythic expression of the same altered-state visions reported by shamans across cultures. In that sense, reading these stories through the ultraterrestrial lens feels as if the Sumerians were documenting contact experiences with beings that slipped between worlds.

Gods, Anunnaki, Apkallu, and Igigi in Mesopotamian Mythology

According to the cuneiform tablets, the divine realm was populated by a complex hierarchy of supernatural beings. At the broadest level, Mesopotamian religion recognized a vast pantheon of gods. These deities were anthropomorphic beings with specific domains, personalities, and mythological roles. However, a quick Google search of "Anunnaki" garners results that are inaccurate. For instance, the search may turn up images of eagle-headed winged beings. These are actually genii, or Apkallu, not Anunnaki. Also, many of the gods were not themselves Anunnaki. While this may seem like hair splitting, it is important to know the difference between the various beings in order to understand how they were categorized, and later misunderstood. Much of what we think we know about the Anunnaki has been shaped by decades of misidentification, mistranslation, and projection.

The Anunnaki

The Anunnaki, often shrouded in mystery and intrigue, are central figures in Mesopotamian mythology, captivating the imagination of those fascinated by ancient civilizations and their strange gods. As beings of immense power and influence, the Anunnaki have long been subjects of speculation, from their roles in divine councils to their associations with the netherworld. The term *Anunnaki* has been interpreted to mean "Those of princely seed" (Finkelstein, 1966). The name appears in various forms in both Sumerian and Akkadian, reflecting its long-standing significance in Mesopotamian culture. Over time, others have interpreted this to mean "those who came from above." The confusion or conflation comes from the way the idea of descending from a higher place is interpreted. Is this descent from a higher place of class position, as in coming from a noble lineage, or is it a descent from a higher physical location like mountains or even the sky?

Throughout different periods, this term has evolved, sometimes referring to the highest gods and, later, to the gods of the underworld. In the earliest Sumerian texts, the Anunnaki represented the highest gods within the Mesopotamian pantheon. The term was also used to denote the pantheon of specific cities, such as the Anunnaki of Eridu or Lagash. However, the exact number and identities of these gods remain unclear. For example, one text mentions "the fifty Anunnaki of Eridu," highlighting that the group could vary depending on the context. A key role of the Anunnaki was deciding fates, a function prominently featured in myths like *Enki and the World Order* (ETCSL 1.1.3). Additionally, in the myth about Inanna's descent into the underworld, the Anunnaki are portrayed as judges, indicating their association with both the heavens and the underworld. Over time, particularly after the Old Babylonian period, the term *Anunnaki* began to signify the gods of the underworld. This shift in meaning contrasted with the term Igigi, which, in some contexts, took on the earlier meaning of Anunnaki as celestial gods.

Although it was once believed that the Anunnaki were not worshiped directly, recent textual evidence suggests otherwise. Ur III period texts indicate that offerings were made to the Anunnaki, albeit sparingly, with only three known attestations in administrative records. The Anunnaki are first mentioned in inscriptions from the post-Akkadian period, such as those of Gudea, and continue to appear in texts up until the Seleucid period. Notably, the Babylonian creation story *Enuma Elish* describes Marduk assigning three hundred Anunnaki gods to the heavens and another three hundred to the netherworld, suggesting a comprehensive structure of divine beings. Ancient texts, such as the *Poem of Erra*, highlight the distinctions and occasional confusion between the Anunnaki and Igigi, demonstrating that these terms had specific and evolving meanings within Mesopotamian mythology.

There is no evidence of temples dedicated solely to the Anunnaki, likely because these gods had individual temples across various cities. Their collective worship may have been more abstract, centered around their roles in divine judgment and fate. Unlike other gods in the Mesopotamian pantheon, there are no known depictions of the Anunnaki as a group. Instead, iconography focuses on individual deities who were part of this collective.

Initially, in Sumerian mythology, the Anunnaki were primarily associated with the underworld and were considered chthonic or earth deities. However, as Mesopotamian religion evolved, particularly in Babylonian times, the concept of the Anunnaki expanded. The Anunnaki came to represent the most important deities in the pantheon, including:

- An/Anu (sky god)
- Enlil (god of wind and earth)
- Enki/Ea (god of wisdom and freshwater)
- Ninhursag (mother goddess)
- Inanna/Ishtar (goddess of love and war)
- Nanna/Sin (moon god)
- Utu/Shamash (sun god)
- Marduk (patron deity of Babylon)

These gods were seen as the divine rulers who decreed the fates of the universe. They were often portrayed as meeting in assembly to make crucial decisions affecting both the divine and mortal realms.

The Apkallu

The Apkallu, in contrast to the Anunnaki, were not gods but rather semi-divine, mythical sages. The term *Apkallu* is Akkadian, derived from the Sumerian *abgal*, meaning "wise" or "sage." In Mesopotamian tradition, there were typically seven Apkallu, associated with the seven antediluvian kings of Sumer. These sages were said to have been created by the god Enki to bring civilization and knowledge to humanity. They were often depicted as half-fish, half-human, symbolizing their connection to Enki's watery realm of wisdom. They bridged the gap between the divine and human realms, facilitating the transfer of divine knowledge to mortal civilization.

The Apkallu were also known as the Mesopotamian fish-men called Oannes, part of a group of demigods (Apkallu in Akkadian, Abgal in Sumerian). The Chaldean scribe Berosus described Oannes as having a fish head along with a second head, the feet of a man, and the tail of a fish, noting that Oannes shared human language but did not consume food (Cory, 1828). The Apkallu, often confused with the Anunnaki, were not gods but rather semi-divine sages. These mythical beings were created by the god Enki to bring wisdom and civilization to humanity. They were considered sources of wisdom and protective entities of wisdom and magic. That they are depicted holding pinecones while anointing kings suggests they were seen as intermediaries between the human and divine realms, capable of facilitating the king's transcendent experiences and divine communications. Their wings reinforce this symbolic interpretation.

Ambicarnate entities are beings that can exist both as spirits and in physical flesh. They are often tied to a specific location, person, or community and offer protection against negative influences, but only if the ritual and moral customs associated with them are observed. These creatures are found in the pagan beliefs of classical antiquity, such as in Greek mythology. In ancient Greek belief, *daimones* (or *daemons*) were considered personal protective spirits and mediators between gods and humans. The word *daemon* comes from the Greek *δαίμων* (*daímōn*), originally referring to the spirit of the departed, or conversely, the departed spirit of the deceased (Greek *σκιά skiá*, meaning "shadow"), the disembodied figures of the dead. According to the Greek philosopher Hesiod, the *daimones* emerged from the souls of people from a past "Golden Age."

Mesopotamian scribes recorded similar beings in their texts, such as the seven sages. The Mesopotamian *Bìt mèseri* cuneiform tablets, which include the *Uruk List of Kings and Sages*, describe the seven sages as the fish-men or Oannes who "were created in the river" and who "ensure the correct execution of the plans of heaven and earth" (Lenzi, 2008). While these beings are depicted as humans dressed as fish, the four tablets of the *Bìt mèseri* text are a newer retelling of the older Uruk List of Kings and Sages, where the seven sages were first depicted as specifically non-human entities. These nonhuman entities were seen as semibiological and ambicarnate, possessing both spiritual and physical qualities.

The Apkallu occupied a unique space between gods and humans, serving as conduits of divine wisdom and guardians of civilization. This complex system of divine beings reflects the rich and nuanced nature of Mesopotamian religious thought, which sought to explain the origins of civilization, the workings of the cosmos, and the relationship between the divine and mortal realms. Hence, the concept of Anunnaki evolved over time and across different Mesopotamian cultures, so the exact membership can vary depending on the specific context and source. Whether gods, ancestors, or ultraterrestrials, their presence shaped the world we inherited.

The Igigi Rebellion and Creation of Humans

Though mentioned less frequently in Sumerian and Babylonian texts, the Igigi play a fascinating role in the mythology. The Igigi were not humans, but rather a lower rank of beings in Mesopotamian mythology. They were a servant class that existed before the creation of humans. Unlike the Anunnaki, who were considered the high-ranking gods, the Igigi were tasked with laborious work, such as digging watercourses and performing other menial tasks.

In some texts, they are described as numbering three hundred, while in others, they are said to be six hundred.

Occasionally, the term *Igigi* is used synonymously with the *Anunnaki*, but this is generally considered incorrect. The *Atra-Hasis* myth, an Akkadian creation story, clearly distinguishes the Igigi from the Anunnaki, depicting them as subordinate beings who bore the brunt of physical labor. The following is a key passage from *Atra-Hasis* that highlights the Igigi as a distinct group of divine beings, separate from the Anunnaki:

> When the gods, man-like,
>
> Bore the labour, carried the load,
>
> The gods' load was great,
>
> The toil grievous, the trouble excessive.
>
> The great Anunnaku, the Seven,
>
> Were making the Igigu undertake the toil.

In some versions of Mesopotamian creation myths, the rebellion of the Igigi led to the creation of humans. Overburdened by their labor, the Igigi revolted against Enlil, one of the head Anunnaki, by burning their tools and surrounding his estate. To resolve this crisis, he created humans to take over the work of the Igigi. Enki was involved in this process. He mixed clay with the blood of a slain god, Kingu, to fashion humans, who then took over the role of laborers previously held by the Igigi.

The Igigi are one of the great mysteries of Mesopotamian mythology. There are few references to them in ancient texts, leading to many questions and much speculation about their true nature and fate. Understanding their story helps us appreciate the complexity and depth of these ancient beliefs. It is particularly interesting to consider that these beings were neither human, nor god, but still a creation of the Anunnaki, leading some modern researchers to believe that they could be related to the alien question.

The Rise of Kings

As Sumerian society grew more complex, new forms of political organization emerged to meet the challenges of urban life. By the Early Dynastic Period (c. 2900–2350 BCE), the independent city-states of Sumer were ruled by powerful dynasties of kings known as *lugals*. These rulers rose to prominence primarily as military leaders, defending their cities against external threats and waging war against rival city-states for control of resources.

The lugals legitimized their authority by positioning themselves as intermediaries between the people and the gods. They claimed divine sanction for their rule and took on the responsibility of ensuring their city's patron deity was properly honored. This fusion of political and religious power is exemplified in the practices of the city state, Ur, where the daughter of the reigning lugal always served as the high priestess of the moon god Sin.

The wealth and power of these early Sumerian rulers is attested to by the magnificent royal tombs discovered at Ur. These elaborate burial chambers, filled with precious goods and the bodies of sacrificed servants, speak to a belief in the enduring nature of royal power even beyond death. The most famous of these early lugals was Gilgamesh of Uruk, whose legendary exploits were immortalized in one of the world's earliest epic poems.

The era of independent Sumerian city-states came to an end around 2300 BCE with the rise of Sargon of Akkad. Sargon united all of Mesopotamia under his rule, creating what is widely regarded as the world's first true empire. The Akkadian Empire, while short-lived, would have a profound impact on the political landscape of the ancient Near East. It demonstrated the possibility of large-scale political unification and set a template for future empires.

The fall of the Akkadian Empire around 2200 BCE ushered in a period of instability and foreign domination. The Gutian people, originally from the Zagros Mountains, seized control of much of Mesopotamia. However, their rule was also relatively short-lived. Around 2120 BCE, the Sumerians reasserted their independence under the leadership of the city-states of Uruk and Ur.

This resurgence of Sumerian power culminated in the establishment of the Third Dynasty of Ur, which once again united all of Sumer under a single rule. The kings of this dynasty, bearing the title King of Sumer and Akkad, presided over a period of renewed cultural flowering. They undertook massive building projects, codified laws, and patronized the arts and sciences. The most famous ruler of this period was Ur-Nammu, renowned both for his military conquests and for promulgating one of the earliest known law codes.

Sumer's Enduring Legacy

The influence of Sumerian civilization extended far beyond the borders of ancient Mesopotamia. As waves of newcomers entered the region—Akkadians, Amorites, Kassites, and others—they invariably adopted and adapted elements of Sumerian culture. The Sumerian language, though it ceased to be spoken in daily life, continued to be used as a language of scholarship and religious ritual for centuries. Sumerian myths, legends, and literary works were preserved and transmitted, influencing the cultural and religious traditions of subsequent civilizations.

The technological and intellectual achievements of the Sumerians laid the groundwork for many of the developments that we associate with later civilizations. Their innovations in agriculture, metallurgy, and urban planning provided the material basis for the growth of complex societies throughout the ancient Near East. Their mathematical and astronomical knowledge, preserved and expanded upon by later cultures, formed the foundation of scientific inquiry for millennia to come.

The story of the Sumerians is, in many ways, the story of civilization itself. From the emergence of the first cities to the development of writing, from the codification of laws to the creation of complex mythologies, their achievements represent a quantum leap in human social organization and intellectual capability, marking the transition from prehistory to history proper. Yet for all their accomplishments, the Sumerians remain in many ways enigmatic. The exact origins of their civilization, the nature of their language (which stands as a linguistic isolate, unrelated to any known language family), and many aspects of their daily lives continue to puzzle scholars. As we continue to decipher their texts and unearth their cities, we are constantly refining our understanding of these remarkable people.

When exploring the origins and influence of the Sumerians and the importance of the Anunnaki, it is essential to recognize that our understanding of these ancient people and gods has been shaped not only by the clay tablets they left behind but, perhaps surprisingly, by the modern forces that sought to control and manipulate their narrative. The story of the Anunnaki, intertwined with that of the Sumerians, has been influenced by more than just ancient myths; it has been colored by the political and academic agendas of those who uncovered these civilizations over a century ago, during the early twentieth century.

Unearthing Empires

The Hidden Agenda

In the scorching heat of the Iraqi desert, where the dust of millennia mingles with the acrid smell of gunpowder, a different kind of battle is being waged. Not with bullets and bombs, but with shovels and brushes. As the echoes of the First World War fade and the Middle East is carved up by European powers, another conquest is underway; the race to control the narrative of human civilization itself.

The year is 1920. Baghdad, the fabled city of *Arabian Nights*, is now under British control. In a small, stuffy office, a woman hunches over a desk strewn with maps and ancient pottery shards. Her name is Gertrude Bell, and she's about to change the course of history—not just for Iraq, but for our understanding of the ancient world. Bell is no ordinary archaeologist. Known as the "Queen of the Desert," she's a spy, a diplomat, and a kingmaker. Now, as the newly appointed Honorary Director of Antiquities for Iraq, she holds the key to unlocking the secrets buried beneath the sand—secrets that powerful men are desperate to control (FO Records, FO 813/1).

What Bell and her colleagues had uncovered was nothing less than evidence of the world's first civilization, the Sumerians, but as this exploration will reveal, the motives behind these excavations were far from purely academic, and the archaeological findings from this period are fraught with controversy and doubt.

To understand the high-stakes game being played out in the deserts of Iraq, we need to wind the clock back a few years. In 1914, German archaeologist Walter Andrae is frantically packing crates at the ancient site of Assur. War is looming, and he knows he must get his precious findings out of the country. Fast forward to 1919, and those same crates are sitting in a Portuguese warehouse, the subject of an international dispute. The British Foreign Office is suspicious. "The amount of money the Germans are willing to spend, viz., £10,000 to keep them out of our hands is very suspicious," one official notes (FO Records, FO 372/873). The million-dollar question may be: Why such interest in old pottery and cuneiform tablets? The answer lies in the power of the past to shape the present. This incident sets the stage for a series of controversies that would plague Mesopotamian archaeology for decades to come, casting a long shadow over the trustworthiness of archaeological claims from this era.

The Great Game of Archaeology

As the dust settled on the First World War, the Middle East became a chessboard for European powers. Archaeology, it turns out, was a crucial piece in this geopolitical game.

"It would be as bad," wrote one British Foreign Office official in 1918, "as the Germans removing the art treasures from Belgium and France." The comparison is telling—ancient artifacts were seen as spoils of war, trophies to be claimed by the victors (FO Records, FO 371/3410).

Yet it was not just about prestige. These relics held a more subtle power—the power to shape narratives, to create founding myths for fledgling nations, and to justify colonial rule. This political dimension of archaeology would lead to numerous instances of misrepresentation and manipulation of findings, eroding the credibility of the field. Enter T. E. Lawrence, better known as Lawrence of Arabia. Like Bell, Lawrence straddled the worlds of archaeology and espionage. His knowledge of ancient sites proved invaluable to British military intelligence. As one Foreign Office document notes, "Most Germans in Iraq have expert knowledge and might prove most useful to their Government in time of war" (FO Records, FO 371/23211). This blurring of lines between archaeology and espionage became a recurring theme, raising questions about the true motivations behind many excavations. The Sumerians represented the dawn of what we think of as civilization, and whoever controlled their narrative could claim to be the inheritors of the very roots of human progress.

This was not lost on the colonial powers scrambling for influence in the region. By emphasizing Iraq's pre-Islamic past, they could weaken pan-Arab and pan-Islamic movements that threatened their control. The manipulation of archaeological findings to suit political agendas would become a hallmark of this era, further undermining the reliability of the historical record. After all, it wasn't just the British who saw the potential in Iraq's ancient past. Nazi Germany, too, had its eyes on Mesopotamia, adding another layer of complexity to the already murky waters of archaeological ethics.

In 1934, a German archaeologist named Julius Jordan was causing quite a stir in Baghdad. Jordan wasn't just any archaeologist—he was the head of the local Nazi party in Iraq. "An archaeological attaché must be unprecedented!" exclaimed Ponsonby Moore Crosthwaite of the British Foreign Office. "But as Dr Jordan has for years been the head of the party in Iraq, the camouflage is painfully thin." Jordan's presence in Iraq was no coincidence. Nazi ideology placed great importance on proving the superiority of the "Aryan race." Mesopotamia, with its ancient civilizations, was seen as a potential birthplace for this supposed master race. "The Nazis were desperate to find evidence that would support their racist theories," explains Jordan. "They saw in the Sumerians a possible 'Aryan' civilization that predated the Semitic Babylonians and Assyrians." This politicization of the past wasn't limited to foreign powers. Local leaders, too, saw the potential in archaeology to shape national identity, further complicating the landscape of archaeological interpretation (FO 371/23202).

The Battle for Iraqi Identity

As Iraq transitioned from British mandate to independent state, archaeology became a battleground for competing visions of

Iraqi identity. Under Sati al-Husri, Iraq's first Director of Antiquities, the focus was on Islamic archaeology, particularly the Abbasid period. This aligned with the pan-Arab ideology prevalent at the time. As Iraqi nationalism grew, so did interest in the pre-Islamic past. The Sumerian civilization, indigenous to Iraq, became a source of national pride. It allowed Iraqis to claim a unique heritage, distinct from both their Arab neighbors and their former British rulers. This shift was not without controversy. As one British official noted in 1939, "Iraqi archaeologists were being trained to excavate Ancient pre-Islamic sites." The implication was clear—archaeology was being used to construct a new national narrative (FO Records, FO 371/23212). This malleability of archaeological interpretation to suit changing political needs casts further doubt on the objectivity of findings from this period.

Perhaps nowhere was the political nature of archaeology more evident than in the fierce battles over where artifacts should be housed. In 1926, Gertrude Bell finally succeeded in establishing the Iraq Museum in Baghdad. But this was just the beginning of a long struggle for control over Iraq's heritage. Western museums, particularly the British Museum, were reluctant to give up their claim to Mesopotamian artifacts. As late as 1935, the Iraqi government was still trying to reclaim the Samarra antiquities from Britain (FO 371/18946). The division of antiquities was a highly contentious issue. It wasn't just about the objects themselves, but about who had the right to interpret and present Iraq's past. These disputes over ownership and control of artifacts highlight the competing interests at play in the field of archaeology, raising questions about the integrity of museum collections and the narratives they present. There was another, more secretive aspect to the archaeological scramble in Iraq—the search for ancient knowledge that could be applied to modern warfare.

The Codebreakers

Leonard Woolley, the famed excavator of Ur, was appointed as archaeological adviser to the War Office during World War II. While officially tasked with protecting ancient sites, there are hints that his expertise was used for more than just preservation (FO 371/37330). "There's a reason why linguists and archaeologists were so prized by intelligence agencies," Jordan explains. "Their skills in decoding ancient languages could be applied to modern cryptography." Indeed, several prominent archaeologists worked as codebreakers during the war. The lines between academic research and military intelligence were often blurred.

As the twentieth century progressed, a new threat emerged—the illegal antiquities trade. The very value placed on Mesopotamian artifacts by Western museums and collectors created a black market that threatened to strip Iraq of its heritage. In 1940, the Iraqi Consul in Washington reached out to the British Embassy, suspecting that antiquities were being smuggled out of Iraq into the United States. The American customs authorities, however, were "unable, or unwilling, to assist" (FO 624/20). This looting would reach its tragic apex in 2003, when the Iraq Museum was infamously pillaged during the US invasion. The echoes of colonial-era disputes over artifact ownership could still be heard in the international outcry and subsequent efforts to repatriate stolen items. The persistence of looting and illegal trade in antiquities serves as a stark reminder of the ongoing challenges in preserving and studying archaeological heritage. It also raises uncomfortable questions about the provenance of many artifacts in Western collections, further eroding trust in the archaeological establishment.

The cumulative effect of these political manipulations, ethical breaches, and outright frauds has been to cast a long shadow over the field of Mesopotamian archaeology. A disturbing question emerges: How much of our understanding of ancient Sumer has been shaped by the political agendas? We have to be critical of the narratives we've inherited. The emphasis on certain aspects of Sumerian civilization may reflect the biases and motivations of early excavators more than historical reality.

Recent scholarship has begun to challenge many long-held assumptions about Sumerian society. The image of Sumer as a precursor to Western civilization is being replaced by a more nuanced understanding of a complex, multicultural society. This ongoing process of revision and reinterpretation underscores the provisional nature of archaeological knowledge and the need for constant critical reassessment. Today, the deserts of Iraq still hold countless secrets. But the political dimension of archaeology hasn't disappeared—it's merely taken on new forms.

Modern Iraq continues to grapple with its archaeological heritage. The destruction of ancient sites by groups like ISIS has shown how the past can still be weaponized in the present. At the same time, Iraqi archaeologists are reclaiming their right to interpret their own history. The reopening of the Iraq Museum and the establishment of new archaeological parks represent a new chapter in Iraq's relationship with its past. Yet the shadow of past controversies looms large, necessitating a cautious approach to new claims and discoveries.

The Peters-Hilprecht Controversy: A Case Study in Archaeological Disputes

One of the most notorious cases that exemplifies the untrustworthiness of early twentieth-century archaeology is the Peters-Hilprecht Controversy, which erupted in the early 1900s. This dispute centered around the excavations at Nippur and the claims made by Hermann Hilprecht about discoveries there. The controversy began when John P. Peters, who had led the first two expeditions to Nippur, accused Hilprecht of misrepresenting findings from the site. Peters alleged that Hilprecht had falsely claimed to have discovered a "Temple Library" at Nippur in 1900 and had misrepresented the provenance of various artifacts in his publications. Key points of contention included these:

- The "Temple Library": Hilprecht claimed to have discovered a vast library of cuneiform tablets in the northeastern part of "Tablet Hill" at Nippur. He described this find in detail, including different departments for education, business, and administration. However, Peters argued that the evidence for this library was dubious at best.
- Misrepresentation of artifacts: Peters demonstrated that several objects Hilprecht had presented as coming from the Temple Library were actually either purchased elsewhere or found in different locations at Nippur years earlier. This included an "Astronomical Tablet" that had been purchased in Baghdad eleven years before the alleged library discovery.
- The Lushtamar tablet: Hilprecht presented a sealed cuneiform tablet addressed to "Lushtamar" as an example of the library's contents. Peters showed that this tablet had actually been purchased, not excavated, and its provenance was highly questionable.
- The jar with the Nippur plan: Hilprecht claimed to have found a jar containing various artifacts, including a clay tablet with a plan of Nippur. However, the expedition's architect, Mr. Fisher, along with Dr. and Mrs. Haynes, contradicted this claim, stating that the plan had been found elsewhere and earlier (Peters, "Nippur Archive," 1908).

Peters argued that these misrepresentations threw doubt on all of Hilprecht's claims about the Nippur excavations. He called for greater transparency and the publication of actual finds from the alleged library. This controversy highlights the potential for abuse in archaeological reporting, especially in an era when few could verify claims made about distant excavations. It underscores the importance of rigorous documentation, peer review, and transparency in archaeological research, elements that were often lacking in early twentieth-century expeditions. Reading these archives left me stunned; the very foundations of Sumerian archaeology were entangled in politics and deception. It made me think that any evidence for ultraterrestrial contact could easily be lost or hidden in the same way. The Peters-Hilprecht Controversy also serves as a cautionary tale about the dangers of sensationalism in archaeology. The allure of dramatic discoveries can sometimes lead to exaggeration or misrepresentation, whether intentional or not. This case emphasizes the need for skepticism and careful verification of archaeological claims, especially when they have implications for our understanding of ancient civilizations (Peters, "Nippur Archive," 1908).

The Arpachiyah Scandal: Unethical Practices in Iraqi Archaeology

Another significant case that undermines the credibility of early twentieth-century archaeology in Iraq is the Arpachiyah Scandal of 1933. This incident involved British archaeologist Max Mallowan, husband of famed mystery writer Agatha Christie, and highlighted the tensions between foreign excavators and Iraqi authorities. Mallowan had been excavating at Arpachiyah, a prehistoric site in northern Iraq, for the British Museum. At the end of the 1932–1933 season, the Director of Antiquities, German archaeologist Julius Jordan, divided up the objects found by various expeditions, as was customary. However, the Minister of Education suddenly intervened, insisting that excavators should only receive duplicates—objects the museum already possessed.

This new instruction effectively meant that excavators couldn't receive anything, as Jordan noted, "for the objects discovered by excavation in 'Iraq were not produced in an age of mass production by machinery and cannot be duplicated" (FO 624/1). The resulting dispute led to a denial of the export permit for Mallowan's finds and sparked international outcry in archaeological circles. This incident marked a turning point in Iraq's control over its antiquities and highlighted the corrupt practices that could arise when political agendas intersected with archaeological research (FO 371/16923).

The Looting of the Iraq Museum

Although it didn't take place in the early twentieth century like previous examples, the looting of the Iraq Museum in 2003 serves as a stark reminder of the ongoing vulnerabilities of archaeological heritage and the long-lasting impacts of earlier controversies and mismanagement. As Baghdad fell during the US invasion of Iraq, the Iraq Museum, home to priceless artifacts spanning thousands of years of Mesopotamian history, was looted. Initially, it was reported that up to 170,000 artifacts had been stolen. While later estimates were lower, the loss was still staggering.

What made this event particularly tragic was evidence suggesting that some of the looting was an inside job. Donny George, the director of research for the State Board of Antiquities and Heritage in Iraq, later revealed that keys to the museum's vaults had gone missing just before the war started. This suggested that some museum staff may have been complicit in the theft (Rothfield, 2009). The looting of the Iraq Museum wasn't just a crime against Iraq, but against world heritage. It highlighted how vulnerable antiquities can be in times of conflict and how corruption can exacerbate the problem. Moreover, it demonstrated the long-term consequences of the contentious history of archaeology in

Iraq, where decades of dispute over ownership and control of artifacts had left the country's heritage in a precarious position.

Tablet Trafficking

A more recent case that illustrates the ongoing problems in the field of Iraqi archaeology is the 2019 incident involving Jim Buckee, a wealthy oil executive, and a collection of ancient cuneiform tablets. Buckee had purchased 154 Mesopotamian cuneiform tablets from a London dealer in 2010 for £1,500 each. However, when he tried to sell the tablets through Christie's auction house in 2019, red flags were raised. Experts noted that the provenance documents for the tablets were suspicious, and it was likely that they had been illegally excavated and smuggled out of Iraq, echoing patterns seen repeatedly since the 2003 US invasion and the catastrophic looting of the Iraq Museum.

The 2003 looting of the Iraq Museum exposed how easily cultural memory can become collateral damage in modern warfare. Thousands of artifacts were stolen, including irreplaceable pieces that embody not only the history of Mesopotamia but also the shared legacy of humanity. There have been a few bright spots amid the ongoing recovery efforts. In 2022, for instance, US federal agents successfully returned two ancient stone artifacts to Iraq: a cuneiform-inscribed tablet fragment and a prism used to teach the cuneiform alphabet, both over four thousand years old. These items were likely looted from Iraq, possibly during the early twentieth century, a time when Mesopotamian archaeology was caught up in the whirlwind of geopolitical and academic intrigue.

The path to recovering these artifacts was anything but straightforward. The tablet came to light after a US buyer picked it up in a 2020 online auction, which led to its seizure by US Customs and Border Protection when it was shipped from the UK without the proper paperwork. As for the cuneiform prism, it was found languishing in a warehouse, when its owner attempted to donate it to an institution without any valid proof of ownership. Fortunately, both artifacts were returned to Iraq, a testament to the ongoing collaboration between Iraqi and American authorities in the mission to repatriate cultural treasures (Kindy, 2022).

This story is part of a much larger, troubling pattern of illegal excavations and artifact theft, which has only intensified during global crises like the Covid-19 pandemic. The illegal antiquities trade continues to be a major hurdle for cultural preservation, with hundreds of thousands of artifacts being seized worldwide in recent years. But despite these challenges, the return of items like these cuneiform tablets and prism offers a glimmer of hope for restoring Iraq's cultural heritage, which has been under constant threat from war, looting, and the black market (Kindy, 2022).

Although the British Museum eventually agreed to oversee the return of the Buckee tablets to Iraq, this case, and other like it, underscores the need for greater due diligence in the antiquities market and highlights the ongoing problem of the illegal antiquities trade and the role wealthy collectors can play in perpetuating it. This story also demonstrates how corruption in the antiquities market often involves a web of actors, from looters on the ground to dealers and collectors in Western countries. The Buckee case serves as a sobering reminder that the problems plaguing Iraqi archaeology are not confined to the past. The allure of ancient artifacts continues to fuel a black market that threatens the integrity of archaeological sites and the ability of scholars to study them in their original context.

The history of archaeology in Iraq, from the early twentieth century to the present day, is a cautionary tale about the intersection of science, politics, and human greed. The Peters-Hilprecht Controversy, the Arpachiyah Scandal, the looting of the Iraq Museum, and the Buckee tablet affair all highlight different facets of the problems that have plagued the field. These incidents reveal a pattern of misrepresentation, manipulation, and outright fraud that has serious implications for our understanding of ancient Mesopotamia. They underscore the need for skepticism when approaching archaeological claims, especially those from the early twentieth century when oversight was limited and political agendas often trumped scientific rigor. Moreover, these controversies highlight the ongoing challenges in preserving and studying archaeological heritage. The illegal antiquities trade continues to threaten sites and museums, while geopolitical conflicts can lead to the destruction or looting of priceless artifacts. It is clear that the power of the past to shape the present is a double-edged sword. While archaeology has the potential to illuminate our shared human heritage, it can also be weaponized to serve political agendas or personal gain. As George Orwell stated in his novel, *1984*: "Who controls the past controls the future: who controls the present controls the past."

The legacy of these controversies calls for a renewed commitment to ethical archaeological practices. This includes rigorous documentation, transparent reporting, and a willingness to subject findings to peer review and scrutiny. It also requires the archaeological community to recognize the rights of host countries to control and interpret their own cultural heritage. For the general public and policymakers alike, these cases serve as a reminder of the need for vigilance. When confronted with sensational archaeological claims or beautiful artifacts of uncertain provenance, it's crucial that we ask critical questions about where these objects came from and how they were obtained.

Despite the controversies and setbacks, the work of uncovering and understanding the past continues. However, the archaeological community must be keenly aware of the ethical pitfalls and potential for abuse that have marred the field in the past, as they proceed with this work. As you walk through the halls of a museum, marveling at artifacts from ancient Sumer, remember the complex history behind their discovery. Each object tells not one story, but two: the tale of the ancient civilization that created it, and the story of how it came to be in that display case, thousands of years and miles from its origin. The next time you read about a sensational archaeological discovery, remember Gertrude Bell in her Baghdad office, and the high-stakes game of empire being played out through the relics of the past. In the world of archaeology, there's always more than meets the eye. The shadows of antiquity are long, and it is only through rigorous scholarship, ethical practice, and constant vigilance that we can hope to illuminate the true stories of our ancient past.

Academic Corruption, Epstein, and the Void

Peer review, long considered the gold standard for quality control in academic publishing, has been a cornerstone of scientific integrity for decades. However, as the landscape of academic publishing has evolved, so too have the challenges and shortcomings of the peer review process. Many argue that it has become corrupted, consolidated, and ultimately ineffective in serving its original purpose.

The concept of peer review can be traced back to the seventeenth century when scientific societies like the Royal Society of London were established. Initially, it was an informal process whereby editors sought advice from knowledgeable colleagues before deciding whether to publish a manuscript. This system gradually evolved over time, becoming more formalized in the twentieth century as academic disciplines expanded and the number of scholarly publications increased.

However, it's crucial to understand that the modern form of peer review, where external experts evaluate manuscripts before publication, is a relatively recent development. Many groundbreaking scientific papers, including Watson and Crick's 1953 paper on the structure of DNA, were published without formal peer review. The editor-driven model, whereby knowledgeable editors took responsibility for the quality of their journals, was the norm for much of scientific publishing's history.

The Robert Maxwell Connection

The transformation of academic publishing in the twentieth century is inextricably linked to Robert Maxwell, a British media mogul whose influence and legacy extend far beyond the confines of academic journals. Maxwell, born Jan Ludvik Hoch in 1923, was a complex and controversial figure who, through sheer ambition and ruthless business practices, built an empire that would profoundly impact the world of academic publishing. Maxwell founded Pergamon Press in 1951, recognizing the growing importance of scientific research in the post–World War II era. He capitalized on the increasing demand for specialized journals, especially as scientific disciplines became more segmented and the volume of research grew exponentially. Under his leadership, Pergamon Press expanded rapidly, acquiring existing journals and launching new ones at an unprecedented rate. This aggressive growth strategy allowed Maxwell to dominate the academic publishing landscape, but it also had far-reaching consequences for the quality and integrity of the peer review process.

Maxwell's approach prioritized rapid expansion and profit over the traditional values of scholarly publishing. This shift began to erode the editor-driven model of quality control that had long been the cornerstone of academic integrity. In its place, Maxwell introduced a more standardized and externalized peer review process, which, while capable of handling the growing volume of submissions, often sacrificed thorough editorial oversight. The emphasis on quantity over quality became a hallmark of the publishing industry under Maxwell's influence, leading to a system that many argue prioritizes commercial interests over the advancement of knowledge. However, Robert Maxwell's legacy extends beyond his direct impact on academic publishing. His life was marked by scandal, espionage, and financial misdeeds, culminating in his mysterious death in 1991. Maxwell's connections to powerful figures and controversial activities have been the subject of much speculation, particularly concerning his family's continued influence.

The Epstein Connection

A particularly dark aspect of Maxwell's legacy is its connection to Jeffrey Epstein, the disgraced financier and convicted sex offender. Ghislaine Maxwell, Robert Maxwell's daughter, became one of Epstein's closest associates. Ghislaine, who was deeply involved in her father's business affairs before his death, transitioned into a role that would later be central to Epstein's criminal activities. She has been accused of recruiting and grooming young girls for Epstein, helping to facilitate the human trafficking network that Epstein operated.

The connection between Robert Maxwell and Epstein is often seen as a continuation of the former's legacy of manipulation, secrecy, and exploitation. While Robert Maxwell focused his efforts on controlling and profiting from the flow of scientific information, his daughter and Epstein leveraged their power and influence to control and exploit vulnerable individuals for their gain. The same ruthlessness and disregard for ethical standards that characterized Robert Maxwell's business dealings appear to have been mirrored in the activities of Epstein and Ghislaine Maxwell. This connection between academic publishing and such criminal activities, while indirect, underscores the dangers of unchecked power and the ways in which influence can be wielded for nefarious purposes. The legacy of Robert Maxwell, therefore, serves as a cautionary tale about the concentration of power in any form, whether in the control of scientific discourse or in the exploitation of human lives.

The legacy of Maxwell's approach, however, extends beyond Pergamon Press. In the decades following Maxwell's innovations, the academic publishing industry has become increasingly consolidated, with a handful of large corporations dominating the market. Giants such as Elsevier, which acquired Pergamon Press in 1991, along with other giants like Wiley and Springer, now control a significant portion of academic journals across various disciplines. This concentration of power has driven up subscription fees, creating barriers to access and slowing the global exchange of knowledge. The financial priorities of these publishers often conflict with the core mission of academic research: the advancement and dissemination of knowledge.

The current peer review system, shaped by this history of rapid expansion and consolidation, faces numerous criticisms such a lack of transparency, bias and conflicts of interest, difficulty in publishing innovative or controversial work, and peer review "rings," to name a few. The consolidation of academic publishing exacerbates many of these issues. With a few major players dominating the market, there's less room for innovation in review processes and a tendency toward homogenization of practices across diverse fields. This one-size-fits-all approach fails to account for the unique needs and norms of different disciplines. The emphasis on journal impact factors and citation metrics as proxies for quality can lead to a focus on sensationalism over solid methodology and a bias toward positive results that may skew the scientific record.

Alien Gods and the Collapse of Trust

When the systems we have placed our trust in begin to falter, it creates a vacuum—a void in which uncertainty and skepticism thrive. This void is often filled not by rigorous inquiry, but by opportunistic and sometimes predatory actors who capitalize on the erosion of trust. These individuals or groups may offer alternative narratives that, while appealing in their novelty or contrarian stance, do not necessarily adhere to the standards of evidence and critical thinking that are foundational to sound scholarship. It is crucial to remember that just because the academic-industrial complex may be flawed, this does not mean that all alternative sources are inherently trustworthy. Critical thinking must remain our guiding principle as we navigate both traditional and alternative avenues of knowledge.

While traditional scholarship views the Anunnaki as just a group of major deities within the Mesopotamian pantheon, part of the myths of a "primitive" pre-science peoples, some alternative researchers have proposed more radical interpretations. In the 1970s, a new, controversial interpretation of the Anunnaki emerged, propelling them into the spotlight of what we now call the ancient astronaut theory. Zecharia Sitchin, an Azerbaijani-born author and self-taught scholar, revolutionized the way we perceive the Anunnaki. His seminal work, *The 12th Planet* (1976), challenged conventional interpretations of Sumerian mythology by proposing that the Anunnaki were not mere deities of myth but actual extraterrestrial beings from a distant planet called Nibiru, which, according to his hypothesis, has an elongated orbit that brings it close to Earth every 3,600 years. According to Sitchin, the Anunnaki arrived on Earth in search of gold, a precious resource they needed to stabilize the atmosphere of their home planet. In this narrative, the Anunnaki used advanced genetic engineering to create humans as a labor force, designed specifically to mine gold for their extraterrestrial masters.

Sitchin's theory is rooted in his interpretation of ancient Sumerian texts, which he claimed to have deciphered differently from mainstream scholars. He argued that the Sumerians possessed advanced knowledge of the solar system and that their myths and legends were, in fact, historical records of extraterrestrial encounters.

This narrative, as Sitchin outlined, not only provides a radical explanation for the origins of humanity but also reinterprets the stories of gods, giants, and demigods found in ancient texts from across the globe. The Great Flood, for instance, which appears in both the Sumerian *Epic of Gilgamesh* and the Bible, is viewed by Sitchin as an event triggered by the Anunnaki, either as a form of population control or as a consequence of their interventions on Earth. Additionally, Sitchin suggested that many of the monumental structures from antiquity, such as the pyramids of Egypt and the ziggurats of Mesopotamia, were built with the guidance or direct assistance of these advanced beings, reflecting their technological prowess.

Despite its popularity among certain groups, Sitchin's work has been met with widespread criticism from historians, archaeologists, and linguists. Many have pointed out that Sitchin's translations of Sumerian and Akkadian texts are inconsistent with accepted scholarly interpretations. Critics also accuse Sitchin of selectively interpreting evidence to fit his narrative, often stretching the meanings of words and phrases beyond their original context.

The Anunnaki Industrial Complex

People all over the world have an interest in understanding the real story of our past and the role gods like the Anunnaki may have played. This has led to many opportunities, as well as challenges, for those navigating the landscape of independent research. No longer are we limited to the official narratives of academia, nor the dissenting views of Sitchin. Many new voices and researchers are working to solve the so-called "Sumerian Problem," a term scholars use to describe the enduring mystery of where the Sumerians came from, how their language fits into known linguistic families, and why their civilization appears to arise so suddenly in the archaeological record. Nevertheless, in the realm of fringe history, some authors have concocted elaborate theories around the Anunnaki that are tied to modern-day schemes that exploit people's fascination with the unknown. It is becoming big business not only to exploit the Anunnaki for financial gain, but also for Hollywood glamor. The latest interpretations are often presented alongside modern-day teachings that mix fringe history with New Age beliefs, such as the law-of-attraction and get-rich-quick schemes.

By connecting ancient alien theories to ideas like manifesting wealth, these narratives exploit people's curiosity and desire for financial success. This exploitation is evident in the way some authors package these theories with promises of accessing hidden truths that can lead to prosperity and empowerment. They often encourage followers to give them money or buy their products to unlock the secrets of the Anunnaki and their supposed influence on human potential. In reality, these commercial offerings often recycle well-worn snake oil, adding little new or substantive information while capitalizing on the allure of the mysterious and the unknown. Clearly, I have nothing against authors and creators monetizing their content, if done in earnest and with ethical clarity.

I spent the first part of my career trying to fight for ethical museum acquisitions and expose the elite power structures behind archaeological excavations. I always followed the money.

While money is always a factor, those in positions of influence may have motivations beyond financial gain to promote the Anunnaki. There is an agenda. It is naïve to think that the world of so-called alternative research is free from the type of maleficence found in the academic industrial complex. I thought the worst instances of the corruption in that realm were clashes of egos, snake oil salesmen, and the occasional tinfoil-hat-wearing paranoid schizophrenic. While there is indeed some of that, I came to learn that the alternative realm itself had been infiltrated by the very groups it had positioned itself to oppose. Perhaps this is by design.

As Mayer Amschel Rothschild, the founder of the Rothschild banking dynasty, has been credited, perhaps falsely, as saying, "Give me control of a nation's money supply, and I care not who makes its laws." There is no primary source for this quote; it was adapted from another well-known quote by Scottish writer and politician, Andrew Fletcher: "Let me make the songs of a nation, and I care not who makes its laws" (Mill, 1867). However, it captures an important idea that posits that often interests behind the scenes control the narrative by controlling money and the creative outputs of a society. To control the narrative, you must also control the opposition. We are living in an age of bot farms, propaganda, and societal unrest. Unfortunately, even the ways people chose to escape or find meaning have not been protected from the trickle-down effect of corruption.

When I explore the Anunnaki, I'm not just looking at their potential extraterrestrial origins or the familiar tales of their quest for gold. My work dives into something more profound—the ways in which the Anunnaki might have shaped our understanding of the world, influenced our spiritual practices, and left a lasting mark on human culture. By examining the archaeological and historical evidence with an open mind, I seek to uncover the messages our ancestors were trying to convey. This journey is about more than just facts; it's about connecting with the deeper, often overlooked aspects of our shared history. Through this lens, I hope to offer a perspective that resonates with those who feel that there's more to our past than what we've been told. To do that, we have to start not at the beginning of civilization, but at the very threshold of human consciousness.

CHAPTER 2

AN EVOLUTIONARY LEAP

New Dawn, Altered States, and Stoned Apes

Man is the most insane species. He worships an invisible God and destroys a visible Nature. Unaware that this Nature he's destroying is this God he's worshiping.

—HUBERT REEVES

The Dawn of Man

In the fertile crescent between the Tigris and Euphrates, ancient Sumerians inscribed on clay tablets a tale that still intrigues us today—the story of the Anunnaki. These otherworldly beings descended from the heavens to bestow knowledge and civilization upon humanity, igniting our imagination and resonating with our quest to understand the dawn of human consciousness.

This Sumerian creation myth speaks of gods creating humans not as mere laborers, but as recipients of divine wisdom. Their myths of the *Enuma Elish* and *Atra-Hasis* recount how the Anunnaki elevated human cognition, reflecting the exponential growth in our species' mental capabilities. Is this ancient narrative literal, or is it a compelling metaphor for the sudden cognitive leaps in human evolution that continue to puzzle scientists and philosophers alike?

The Anunnaki's influence on early human cognition may give clues about those sudden evolutionary leaps. The narrative of these divine beings bestowing knowledge may not only serve as mythological lore but could indeed reflect an actual event in humanity's cognitive development. Both can be true at the same time, but this would challenge the conventional understanding of early human societies, positioning the Anunnaki as catalysts in the transition from primal to civilized man.

The theme of divinely gifted knowledge is not a new idea, nor is it held only by the Sumerians. It echoes across cultures and epochs. Greek mythology gives us Prometheus, stealing fire from the gods to enlighten humanity. The Biblical Garden of Eden presents the tree of knowledge, whose fruit forever alters human awareness. These stories, though separated by vast distances and centuries, converge on a singular idea: the abrupt expansion of human consciousness (Hamilton, 1942). The parallels between ancient myths and contemporary art prompt us to consider: Could these narratives be allegorical representations of actual evolutionary leaps in our cognitive past? This intriguing question propels us into the realm of scientific theories that attempt to illuminate the nature and development of human consciousness. The fossil and archaeological evidence of human prehistory reveals several interrelated patterns. Brain size tripled from ape-level equivalence beginning 2.5 million years ago, possibly in several bursts.

Stone tool technology emerged at the same time, increasing in sophistication through step-like changes, but characterized by long plateaus that lacked innovation. Only within the past one hundred thousand years did our ancestors' technical repertoire display humanlike innovation. During this same period, the first evidence of symbolic behavior appeared, including body ornamentation, art, and ritualized burial.

These later, dramatic changes in human behavior, sometimes called "the big bang" of human culture, may be key to understanding the origin of the modern human mind. Scientists have proposed that the human mind passed through three stages during prehistory. The first stage, lasting until about 2.5 million years ago when the first *Homo* species evolved, was characterized by generalized intelligence. In the second stage, specialized realms of intelligence developed, including social, and technical intelligence, operating independently (the "Swiss Army knife" view of the mind). The third stage saw the emergence of cognitive fluidity, linking these separate intelligences and leading to the creativity of the modern human mind that ignited the big bang of human culture. The concept of cognitive fluidity, proposed by cognitive archaeologist Steven Mithen, refers to the ability to combine different types of thinking—such as social, technical, and natural history intelligence—in creative ways (Mithen, 1996). The abruptness of this change mirrors the sudden impartation of knowledge by the Anunnaki in Sumerian myths, raising the possibility that ancient storytellers were capturing, in metaphorical terms, a real evolutionary event, but what if our ancestors' mental experiences differed fundamentally from our own? Almost all ancient texts speak of a time when the gods were a very present part of the lives of humans. In what seems to be a godless postmodern, even posthuman, landscape, the shine of this Golden Age has dimmed, lost to the weight of time. Perhaps a glimmer is still waiting to be rediscovered.

The Lesson

The lecture hall bustled with students settling in.

"Welcome," I said, silencing the chatter. "Today, we embark on a journey through time, space, and the human mind." I stood at the podium, outwardly composed in my blazer and glasses. With a click of my remote, the lights dimmed. Suddenly, the thunderous opening notes of Richard Strauss's "Also sprach Zarathustra" filled the auditorium. The iconic "dun dun dun dun dun" of the kettle drums reverberated through the space as the opening scene of Stanley Kubrick's *2001: A Space Odyssey* illuminated the screens.

I watched my students' faces as the music swelled, I walked to the front, shadows playing off the projector's glow. Their expressions ranged from confusion to awe to dawning curiosity. Perfect.

As the lights rose, I stepped from behind the podium. "We're here to explore the big questions: Who are we? Where do we come from? And where are we going?" I paused. "Or, to put it another way: Where are the Gods?"

A student in the front row leaned forward, captivated. If only he knew how literal that question had become in my investigations.

"Today, we'll begin with one of the most provocative statements in modern philosophy." I turned and wrote on the board: "GOD IS DEAD."

Facing the class again, I saw a mix of shock, intrigue, and thoughtfulness. It was 8:00 a.m., but they were now awake.

"These words, penned by Friedrich Nietzsche, encapsulate a central theme in both his philosophy and the esoteric teachings of the Mystery Schools: the evolution of human consciousness beyond traditional religious constructs toward self-realized divinity."

As I continued, I felt the familiar thrill of unveiling knowledge, igniting sparks of curiosity that could grow into a relentless pursuit of hidden truths. I valued the academic freedom at my small state college, inspiring and challenging students in ways few institutions would permit. My teaching philosophy echoed Plutarch: "Education is the kindling of a flame, not the filling of a vessel." This flame, once lit, has the power to illuminate even the darkest corners of human understanding.

> *God is dead. God remains dead. And we have killed him. How shall we comfort ourselves, the murderers of all murderers? What was holiest and mightiest of all that the world has yet owned has bled to death under our knives: who will wipe this blood off us? What water is there for us to clean ourselves? What festivals of atonement, what sacred games shall we have to invent? Is not the greatness of this deed too great for us? Must we ourselves not become gods simply to appear worthy of it? (Nietzsche, 1989)*

This profound statement encapsulates a central theme in both Nietzsche's philosophy and the esoteric teachings of what are known as the Mystery Schools: the evolution of human consciousness beyond traditional religious constructs and toward a state of self-realized divinity. Friedrich Nietzsche, a nineteenth-century German philosopher, profoundly influenced modern thinking with his radical ideas about morality, religion, and human potential. His concept of the Übermensch, introduced in his seminal work, *Thus Spoke Zarathustra*, envisions a future where humanity evolves beyond its current state, embracing a life-affirming philosophy and creating new values in a world without traditional religious frameworks. In our modern era, this ancient theme found new life in Stanley Kubrick's groundbreaking film *2001: A Space Odyssey* (1968). Kubrick's mysterious monolith serves as a cinematic analog to the Anunnaki, an external force catalyzing human evolution. Both represent the mysterious spark that ignites profound changes in human cognition and capabilities. The visual metaphor of the monolith in the film aligns with Friedrich Nietzsche's concept of the Übermensch, or "superman"—a vision of humanity transcending its current limitations to achieve a higher state of being (Nietzsche, 1989; 2003).

Kubrick's choice of Richard Strauss's "Also sprach Zarathustra" ("Thus Spoke Zarathustra") as the film's opening music is no coincidence. Strauss's tone poem, inspired by Nietzsche's philosophical novel of the same name, provides a musical embodiment of humanity's evolutionary journey. The iconic opening fanfare, with its ascending perfect fifths, musically represents the ascent of consciousness that Kubrick visually portrays on screen. As the powerful strains of Strauss's composition fill our ears, we are presented with a striking cosmic alignment: Earth, Moon, and Sun. This celestial dance sets the stage for humanity's grand evolutionary drama, echoing Nietzsche's call for mankind to strive beyond its current limitations.

The film opens with a dark, spherical object slowly descending from the top of the screen, revealing itself to be the Earth. Behind it, we see the moon, and as both celestial bodies sink lower, the sun dramatically emerges. This celestial alignment forms the shape of the "boat of Isis," a powerful symbol in ancient Egyptian mythology. In secret arcane teachings, this imagery represents the cosmic dance of creation. The alignment of Earth (representing the material world), the moon (symbolizing hidden knowledge or the feminine principle), and the sun (embodying divine consciousness or the masculine principle) signifies the moment of cosmic awakening, the birth of a new age of consciousness. It visually echoes Nietzsche's question: "Must we ourselves not become gods?"

As the sun rises over a desolate, prehistoric landscape, we witness the first stirrings of life. This barren world, slowly awakening to the sun's life-giving rays, symbolizes the primordial state of human consciousness; empty, yet full of potential. The rising sun, a universal symbol of enlightenment and divine wisdom in many ancient traditions, heralds the coming transformation, much like Nietzsche's Zarathustra descending from his mountain to bring enlightenment to humanity.

With the sun's journey across the sky, we see the gradual appearance of plant and animal life, culminating in the emergence of our ape-like ancestors. This progression symbolizes the Mystery School belief in the evolutionary nature of consciousness, from its most basic forms to increasingly complex and self-aware states. It is a visual representation of the long journey from Nietzsche's proclamation of God's death to humanity's potential ascension to godhood.

The appearance of the black monolith is perhaps the most enigmatic and symbolically charged moment in the sequence. In the context of Mystery School teachings and Nietzsche's philosophy, the monolith can be interpreted as the embodiment of the challenge posed by the death of God. It represents the void left by the loss of traditional belief systems and the opportunity for a new, self-directed evolution of consciousness.

Following the monolith encounter, we witness one ape's epiphany in using a bone as a tool and weapon. This leads to the first act of intergroup violence, the "first murder." This sequence symbolizes humanity's double-edged gain of knowledge: the ability to better ensure survival, but also the capacity for destruction. It echoes Nietzsche's words: "What was holiest and mightiest of all that the world has yet owned has bled to death under our knives." This imagery hints at the death of God as being one of a blood sacrifice.

The famous match-cut from the thrown bone to an orbiting satellite encapsulates both the Mystery School view of human evolution and Nietzsche's concept of mankind's potential. In a single edit, we leap from humanity's first tool to its most advanced technology, suggesting that all human progress stems from that initial awakening of consciousness—the first step toward becoming "worthy" of the death of God. Kubrick's "The Dawn of Man" sequence, underscored by Strauss's Nietzsche-inspired composition, serves as a powerful visual allegory for both Mystery School teachings and Nietzschean philosophy on the evolution of human consciousness. From cosmic alignments to the monolith's catalyst, from the first tool to space-faring technology, the sequence encapsulates key esoteric concepts about humanity's journey from unconscious matter to self-aware beings capable of contemplating their own origins and destiny. Should we not consider our role in this cosmic drama and our potential to "become gods" in the face of a universe devoid of traditional divinity? What if the gods are not dead after all? What if we just stopped listening?

The Mysterious Leap

The Ancestors

Can you remember the voice of your mother calling you to dinner? Would you confuse the memory of her voice with her actual voice, speaking to you in real time? Perhaps the ancients could not discern the memory of a voice from the actual voice? According to American psychologist and researcher Julian Jaynes's controversial theory of the bicameral mind, this may explain not only ancestor worship, but the origin of "the gods" (Jaynes, 1976). His theory offers a fascinating perspective on the development of human consciousness. Jaynes proposed that ancient humans experienced a split consciousness, with one part of the mind issuing commands that the other part interpreted as the voices of gods or ancestors. This theory, in which he posited that early humans experienced thoughts as auditory hallucinations attributed to gods or ancestors, provides a provocative lens through which to interpret Sumerian accounts of communication with the Anunnaki. Perhaps the "voices of the gods" in ancient texts are descriptions of this bicameral mental state.

Jaynes's theory suggests that the consciousness we now take for granted (our internal dialogue, self-awareness, capacity for abstract thought, etc.) is a relatively recent development in human history, perhaps only a few thousand years ago. This radical reconceptualization of ancient minds offers a fresh lens through which to examine the puzzles of our past and the possibilities of our future. The voices of gods in ancient texts might be the echoes of a mode of consciousness alien to our modern minds, yet integral to our cognitive heritage. He argued that ancient humans, including those who built complex civilizations and possessed seemingly advanced knowledge, operated under a different cognitive framework. This bicameral consciousness, as Jaynes termed it, involved a mind divided into two chambers: one that issued commands and another that perceived these directives as external, often divine, voices.

This theory offers a novel perspective on the perplexing aspects of ancient cultures we've encountered. The Dogon people of Mali, for example, have long been cited in alternative literature for their alleged knowledge of the Sirius star system and their oral traditions describing amphibious beings called the Nommo, said to have descended from the sky. The universal themes in mythologies across disparate civilizations, the recurring motifs of gods imparting knowledge to humanity, and even the Dogon's claimed communication with the Nommo beings might all be understood as expressions of this bicameral mentality. In this light, the voices of gods and ancestors in ancient texts could be interpreted not as metaphorical or purely fictional accounts, but as genuine experiences of a consciousness structured differently from our own. Jaynes's hypothesis challenges us to reconsider our assumptions about the continuity of human cognitive experience. If consciousness as we know it is indeed a recent emergence, how might this reshape our understanding of ancient wisdom and capabilities? Furthermore, if human consciousness has undergone such a profound transformation in relatively recent history, what does this suggest about its potential for future evolution? The gods themselves may simply be an epiphenomena of the brain as it enters into a new phase of cognitive evolution.

Catching Fire

Richard Wrangham offered a rather straightforward hypothesis that suggests that the advent of cooking played a crucial role in human brain development. Wrangham, a British primatologist and biological anthropologist, is a professor at Harvard University. He has extensively studied primate behavior and its implications for understanding human origins, which he discussed in his groundbreaking work, *Catching Fire: How Cooking Made Us Human* (2009). Wrangham's research continues to shape the fields of anthropology and evolutionary biology, offering new insights into the links between diet, cognition, and the development of human society.

By making food more easily digestible and increasing its caloric value, cooking allowed our ancestors to devote less energy to digestion and more to brain growth (Wrangham, 2009). While proponents of a raw diet may argue for the health of their approach, cooking plant-based foods acts as a form of predigestion by breaking down the robust cellular structures that encapsulate nutrients. These cell walls, primarily composed of cellulose and other complex carbohydrates, present a significant challenge to the human digestive system. When plants are consumed raw, many nutrients remain sequestered within these cellular matrices, as human digestive enzymes often lack the capacity to fully penetrate these structures.

The application of heat during cooking induces structural changes in plant tissues, partially degrading cell walls and disrupting cellular compartmentalization. This thermal processing enhances the accessibility of intracellular nutrients to digestive processes, effectively increasing their bioavailability. As a result, the digestive system can more efficiently extract and absorb essential vitamins, minerals, and other bioactive compounds. This enhanced nutrient extractability leads to improved absorption kinetics in the gastrointestinal tract, ensuring that a greater proportion of nutrients enter the bloodstream rather than passing through the body unutilized. In essence, cooking serves as a preliminary phase of digestion, optimizing nutrient uptake and thereby maximizing the nutritional benefits derived from plant-based foods. This theory provides a concrete, physical complement to the more esoteric explanations of consciousness development.

Stoned Apes

Venturing into more controversial territory, we find Terence McKenna's stoned ape theory. McKenna was an American ethnobotanist, mystic, and author, best known for his advocacy of the exploration of altered states of consciousness through the use of psychoactive plants. His work, including his influential book *Food of the Gods* (1992), proposed the stoned ape theory, suggesting that the consumption of psilocybin mushrooms by early hominids played a significant role in the evolution of human consciousness. Although controversial, his ideas had a lasting impact on the study of consciousness and the role of psychedelics in human culture. McKenna's unique blend of science, mysticism, and speculation continues to inspire discussions about the boundaries of human cognition and the nature of reality.

This theory gains particular relevance when considered alongside the rich history of entheogen use in ancient cultures, including Mesopotamia. The idea that consciousness-altering substances played a role in our cognitive evolution offers a potential bridge between the mystical experiences described in ancient texts and the biological mechanisms of brain development. As outlandish as it may sound at first, it is worth considering how such transformative experiences could have attributed to accounts of divine intervention in mythology and might, in fact, have a neurochemical basis.

The Psychedelic Connection

The psychedelic connection to the Anunnaki and human consciousness evolution isn't just a relic of ancient history; it may offer a radical reinterpretation of human history and potential. Perhaps the seeds of our future evolution may lie not in the stars, but in the unexplored realms of our own consciousness. Modern research into psychedelic substances, particularly DMT (N,N-Dimethyltryptamine), has uncovered striking parallels between contemporary psychedelic experiences and ancient accounts of divine encounters. DMT, often called the "spirit molecule," is a powerful psychedelic compound found naturally in many plants and animals, including humans. When consumed, it can induce profound alterations in consciousness, often characterized by encounters with seemingly autonomous entities (McKenna, 1992).

These DMT-induced entity encounters bear uncanny resemblances to descriptions of Anunnaki interactions in ancient Mesopotamian texts. Participants in DMT studies often report meeting beings of great wisdom and power, existing in realms beyond ordinary reality. These entities are frequently described as teachers or guides, imparting knowledge and insights that transform the experiencer's understanding of reality and consciousness (Luke, 2011). The parallels to the Anunnaki, who were said to have bestowed knowledge and civilization upon humanity, are hard to ignore, but what if these similarities aren't mere coincidence? What if the ancient Mesopotamians, through their use of psychedelic substances, were accessing the same realms of consciousness that modern DMT users report?

The exploration of psychedelic substances used to achieve altered states of consciousness has long intrigued both the ancient and modern world. These substances, some now referred to as *entheogens*—a term coined in 1979 by a group of ethnobotanists including Carl A. P. Ruck, Richard Evans Schultes, and R. Gordon Wasson—are derived from the Greek word *entheos*, which relates to divine inspiration. This term reflects the belief that these substances can facilitate a connection with the divine or the spiritual world, akin to the mystical experiences described in the ancient Mysteries of Dionysus (Ruck et al., 1979).

The rebranding of hallucinogens as entheogens emerged as a way to move away from the negative connotations associated with terms like *hallucinogen* and *psychedelic*. The former was linked to delirium and insanity, while the latter had become synonymous with the counterculture excesses of the 1960s. The shift toward the use of *entheogen* was part of a broader movement that redefined the role of these substances in spiritual and psychological exploration. This redefinition coincided with changes in psychiatry, where figures like R. D. Laing, a prominent "anti-psychiatrist," suggested that mental illness could be viewed as a transformative experience rather than merely a breakdown. Laing's ideas, which drew comparisons between schizophrenic episodes and shamanic journeys, resonated with the founders of the Esalen Institute in

Big Sur, California—a place deeply intertwined with the rise of the New Age movement and the Human Potential Movement (Boekhoven, 2011).

Esalen, established in 1962 with the help of Aldous Huxley, became a hub for those exploring new frontiers of consciousness. It hosted a variety of thinkers who were instrumental in shaping the counterculture of the 1960s and beyond. The institute's founders, Michael Murphy and Richard Price, envisioned a place that transcended the limitations of mainstream academia, where experimentation with various philosophies, religious disciplines, and psychological techniques could flourish. Influential figures like R. Gordon Wasson, Robert Anton Wilson, Terence McKenna, and others found a platform at Esalen to explore and disseminate ideas about entheogens and their potential to unlock human potential (Kripal, 2007).

The Esalen Institute's influence on the counterculture and the New Age movement cannot be overstated. It was a crucible for the development of humanistic psychology and neoshamanism, a modern form of shamanic practice that often incorporated the use of entheogens. Esalen's impact extended beyond the hippie movement, affecting broader societal changes and shaping how individuals understood their inner lives and potential. This was part of a larger cultural shift, where the personal liberation of the 1960s began to be viewed as a path to broader social change, a concept that resonated deeply with those who turned away from traditional politics in favor of inner transformation (Curtis, 2002).

Entheogens played a central role in this transformative period. The idea that these substances could generate divine experiences or facilitate contact with higher realms became integral to the practices and beliefs that flourished at places like Esalen. The term *entheogen* encapsulated the potential of these substances to reveal hidden dimensions of consciousness, whether through personal spiritual experiences or as tools for psychological healing and growth. Figures like Timothy Leary, who popularized the use of LSD, also became associated with the exploration of entheogens. Leary's experiments, along with those of his contemporaries, opened the door to broader acceptance of these substances as means to expand consciousness. This movement was not without controversy, but it also spurred significant interest in the potential of psychedelics to bring about profound personal and societal change. The connection between psychedelics and spiritual awakening was further explored by individuals such as Terence McKenna, who posited that the ingestion of psychedelic mushrooms played a crucial role in human evolution, hence, his stoned ape theory (McKenna, 1992).

The role of the Esalen Institute in nurturing these ideas cannot be understated. It provided a space where the exploration of altered states of consciousness through entheogens was not only accepted but encouraged as a path to personal and collective enlightenment. The institute's focus on blending Eastern and Western philosophies, along with its openness to experimental psychology, made it a unique environment for ideas to develop that continue to influence contemporary thought on spirituality and consciousness.

Entheogens have also been linked to the concept of the *Omega Point*, a term popularized by Pierre Teilhard de Chardin, which refers to the ultimate goal of evolution as a point of divine unification. This idea, along with others related to the evolution of consciousness, found fertile ground at Esalen, where thinkers like Stanislav Grof developed transpersonal psychology, a field that integrates spiritual experiences with psychological practices. Grof's work, particularly his development of Holotropic Breathwork, provided a non-drug alternative to achieve altered states of consciousness, further expanding the ways in which individuals could explore the depths of the mind and spirit (Grof, 1985).

As the exploration of entheogens continued, their role in modern spiritual practices became more deeply embedded in the fabric of the New Age and Human Potential movements. These substances, once relegated to the fringes of society, gained recognition as powerful tools for spiritual awakening and psychological healing. Whether through the ancient rites of the mysteries or the modern practices, entheogens remain a powerful tool for those seeking to expand their understanding of the mind and spirit.

The realms encountered in psychedelic states, including those populated by Anunnaki-like entities, could be understood as alternative ontological frameworks—*not* hallucinations or fantasies, but glimpses into aspects of reality typically hidden from ordinary perception. This ontological approach to psychedelic experiences and Anunnaki encounters finds support in the work of anthropologist Michael Harner. Through his extensive research into shamanic practices across cultures, Harner developed the concept of *core shamanism*, which posits that there are fundamental similarities in the techniques and experiences of shamans worldwide, regardless of their cultural context (Harner, 1990). These commonalities suggest a universal aspect to altered states of consciousness, one that transcends cultural boundaries and points to a shared reality accessible through these states.

The Anunnaki, viewed through this shamanic lens, could be understood as emanations of this universal consciousness—archetypal beings that emerge when human awareness expands beyond its ordinary limits. This interpretation aligns with Carl Jung's concept of the collective unconscious and its archetypes, suggesting that the Anunnaki might represent universal patterns of psychic energy that manifest in similar forms across cultures and time periods (Jung, 1960). In fact, certain interpretations of quantum physics, particularly the many-worlds interpretation proposed by Hugh Everett III, suggest that all possible alternate histories and futures are real, each representing an actual "world" or "universe" (Everett, 1957). In this context, the realms encountered in psychedelic states that may be populated by Anunnaki-like entities could be understood as glimpses into parallel realities or dimensions normally inaccessible to our ordinary consciousness. The implications of this quantum-inspired interpretation are staggering. It suggests that the Anunnaki myths might be more than just stories or even representations of psychedelic experiences. These could be accounts of actual interactions with beings from parallel realities. This doesn't mean that the Anunnaki are literally extraterrestrial visitors in the conventional sense, but rather transdimensional entities accessible through altered states of consciousness.

The cuneiform tablets describing the Anunnaki and their interactions with humanity take on new layers of meaning when viewed through this lens. The cuneiform writing system itself, with its complex symbols and multiple levels of meaning, mirrors the multifaceted nature of psychedelic experiences. Each cuneiform sign, like each aspect of a psychedelic vision, can be read on multiple levels—literal, symbolic, and cosmic.

The Anunnaki, then, are not distant, unknowable beings, but integral aspects of our own consciousness, perhaps even catalysts of the evolutionary process. Moreover, this interpretation of the Anunnaki as aspects of expanded consciousness accessed through various means, including psychedelics, challenges the purely biological concept of human evolution. Rather than a material process or one guided by external, extraterrestrial intervention, human evolution could be seen as a journey of consciousness expansion. The "gifts" of the Anunnaki—writing, mathematics, agriculture, and other foundations of civilization—might represent insights gained through altered states of consciousness, translated into practical innovations that transformed human society.

This phenomenon of receiving "downloads" of information or encountering inexplicable "technologies" in psychedelic states bears a striking resemblance to the Mesopotamian concept of the *me*—the divine decrees or blueprints of civilization bestowed by the Anunnaki. The *me* were thought to contain the essences of all aspects of human culture and cosmic order, from abstract concepts like justice and truth to practical skills like metalworking and animal husbandry (Kramer, 1963). The parallels suggest that both ancient Mesopotamians and modern psychonauts may be accessing similar realms of expanded consciousness, interpreting their experiences through the cultural and conceptual frameworks available to them.

Psychedelic Gateways to Anunnaki Consciousness

This framework, where gods descended to impart wisdom, may reflect more than just ancient storytelling; it might be a record of a pivotal moment in human evolution. The journey from mere survival to the complex development of urban centers parallels the sudden leaps in cognitive capacity that have baffled scientists and scholars alike, leading many to conclude that the Anunnaki could only be extraterrestrial in nature. But, what if the Anunnaki were not gods, nor extraterrestrials, as sci-fi films would depict, but instead be something else altogether? Could the true nature of the Anunnaki be not extraterrestrial, but ultraterrestrial? From the caves of prehistory to the frontiers of neuroscience, we might reconsider the nature of these beings. The advanced knowledge and technologies attributed to the Anunnaki could be understood as insights gained through altered states of consciousness, translated into cultural and technological innovations that propelled human civilization forward.

To support such claims, I knew I would need more evidence. As I pored over ancient texts in the dim light of my study, a startling connection between the Anunnaki and psychedelics began to crystallize. My fingers traced the outlines of mushroom-shaped cuneiform tablets depicted in a dog-eared archaeology journal. Could these ancient artifacts hold the key to unlocking a mystery that has puzzled scholars for centuries? The link between the Anunnaki and human consciousness, I realized, was deeply intertwined with sacred plant medicine, stretching back to the dawn of civilization. Archaeological evidence and ancient texts supported this hypothesis, but it was the unusual Uruk mushroom tablets that truly captured my imagination.

The story of the Anunnaki and human consciousness is inextricably linked to the realm of psychedelics, a connection that stretches back to the very dawn of civilization. This hypothesis is not mere speculation; it's rooted in archaeological evidence and ancient texts that have long puzzled scholars. The discovery of the Uruk mushroom tablets in the early twentieth century provides a glimpse into this ancient relationship between humanity, the divine, and mind-altering substances (Frahm, 2013). In 1912–13, German archaeologists unearthed over seventy clay objects shaped like mushrooms in the ancient city of Uruk, located in present-day Iraq. These *Tonpilze*, or clay mushrooms, were found in a kiln within the palace of King Sîn-kāšid, who ruled around 1865–33 BCE. Far from being mere curiosities, these tablets were inscribed with Sumerian cuneiform, containing royal boasts about temple construction and offering formulas for the gods' favor (Frahm, 2013). What is most intriguing, these mushroom-shaped missives were meant to be hidden within temple walls, out of human sight—a direct line of communication with the divine. This practice bears a striking resemblance to the modern Jewish tradition of placing small pieces of paper containing written prayers into the cracks of the Western Wall in Jerusalem, also known as the Wailing Wall. In both cases, we see a deeply human desire to establish a private, physical connection with the divine, in a space hidden from mortal eyes but believed to be directly accessible to the gods. This parallel suggests a continuity in human religious behavior across vast stretches of time and cultural divides, highlighting the enduring nature of our quest to communicate with the transcendent. The deliberate shaping of these tablets into mushroom forms and their secretive placement within sacred spaces suggests a purpose beyond mere record-keeping or even royal propaganda. It hints at a deeper, more mystical significance, one that aligns with the idea of mushrooms as conduits of divine communication.

Still, the Uruk mushroom tablets are just one piece of a much larger puzzle. John Allegro, a maverick scholar and one of the original translators of the Dead Sea Scrolls, proposed a theory so controversial it nearly ended his academic career. In his book *The Sacred Mushroom and the Cross*, Allegro argued that early Christianity, far from being the root of Western religious tradition, was itself the product of an ancient fertility cult centered around the use of psychedelic mushrooms (Allegro, 1970). Allegro's work, though widely dismissed at the time, takes on new significance when viewed through the lens of modern psychedelic research and our evolving understanding of consciousness. He pointed out numerous linguistic connections between ancient Sumerian and later Semitic languages, arguing that many religious terms and concepts could be traced back to code words for mushrooms and sexual practices. While his specific arguments about Christianity remain contentious, his broader insight, that ancient religions were intimately connected with altered states of consciousness induced by psychedelic substances, aligns with a growing body of evidence from various cultures around the world (Ruck et al., 2001).

The recurring motif of a sacred plant or substance that confers divine knowledge or immortality, like the amrita of Hindu mythology or the golden apples of the Norse gods, may well be a cultural memory of these psychedelic experiences (McKenna, 1992). In the context of the Anunnaki, this psychedelic connection takes on profound implications. If these beings were indeed communicating with humans through altered states of consciousness, it suggests a mode of interaction far more complex and nuanced than the idea of physical, extraterrestrial visitors. Instead, it points to the possibility of the Anunnaki as aspects of a higher dimensional reality, accessible through the portal of the human mind when it's expanded beyond its ordinary limits. Could this be the real meaning of *stargates*?

This is perhaps the most challenging and controversial take on the Anunnaki because it challenges not only the mainstream academic consensus, but also the alternative viewpoints that have made their way into pop-culture. Imagine, for a moment, that the Anunnaki are neither alien nor divine, but aspects of cosmic consciousness itself, a bridge between the material and the mystical, the scientific and the spiritual. This revolutionary perspective doesn't just reframe our understanding of these ancient beings, it opens doorways to new realms of human potential and cosmic connection. From the mushroom-shaped tablets of ancient Uruk to modern encounters with DMT-induced "machine elves," a striking pattern emerges. These altered states of consciousness offer glimpses into realms beyond ordinary perception, realms that bear uncanny resemblances to ancient accounts of Anunnaki encounters.

Reconceptualizing the Anunnaki as manifestations of expanded consciousness challenges us to explore the neurological aspects of these profound experiences. If these entities are accessed through altered states, we must ask: What occurs in the brain during these encounters? Recent advancements in neuroscience provide fascinating insights into the mechanics of psychedelic experiences, offering potential explanations for the neurological basis of such cosmic connections. By exploring how these substances impact brain function, we might uncover the biological mechanisms that enable encounters with Anunnaki-like entities or realms.

The brain itself becomes a battleground of revelation as neuroscience grapples with the profound alterations in consciousness induced by substances like DMT. These experiences, often described in terms strikingly similar to encounters with the Anunnaki and other mythological beings, blur the lines between internal and external realities. Are these entities mere products of neurochemistry, or do psychedelics act as technological tools, or evolutionary catalysts, fine-tuning the human brain to perceive aspects of reality normally hidden from view?

Recent fMRI studies on psychedelic experiences have yielded surprising results. Contrary to expectations of increased brain activity, researchers found that psilocybin actually decreased activity in key brain network hubs. Robin Carhart-Harris and his colleagues discovered reduced blood flow to the thalamus, anterior and posterior cingulate cortex, and medial prefrontal cortex (2012). This "quieting" of typically hyperactive regions, particularly in the default mode network, may explain the profound alterations in consciousness associated with psychedelic experiences. The study suggests that the brain's organizational principles are disrupted by psilocybin, "creating a state of unconstrained cognition" (Carhart-Harris et al., 2012).

The ancient Sumerians left textual evidence of their cognition and they were certainly cooking their food. Were these two advantages alone what sparked their innovation? They claim it was the coming of the Anunnaki. The Sumerians may have held secrets far more profound than their famous cuneiform writing, cooked food, or even stepped ziggurats. According to the controversial theories of Allegro, these ancient people were the progenitors of a sacred tradition centered around the use of psychoactive mushrooms, particularly the striking red-and-white spotted *Amanita muscaria*. Allegro's work suggests that the Sumerians viewed these mushrooms not merely as interesting flora, but as gateways to divine realms. In his interpretation, the vivid and often surreal nature of Sumerian mythology finds its source in the altered states of consciousness induced by these powerful fungi. The fantastical beasts, the interactions with gods, the journeys to other worlds—all of these, Allegro proposes, may have sprung from minds expanded by psilocybin. But is there any archaeological evidence to support Allegro's claims?

In the Southern Levant, evidence of an ancient mushroom cult has indeed emerged, predating Sumerian civilization. Archaeologist Estelle Orrelle's research reveals a complex spiritual tradition spanning from the late Holocene to the Early Bronze Age (Orrelle, 2022). This discovery reshapes our understanding of pre-Sumerian religious practices and their potential influence on later cultures. The Negev and Sinai desert rock art, for example, display intriguing motifs: round-headed figures and stick-and-circle shapes likely representing mushrooms (Orrelle, 2022). These images resonate with psychedelic art found in other ancient cultures, suggesting widespread entheogen use. Orrelle's interpretation of ibex imagery offers a novel perspective on human-animal-fungus relationships. Depictions of male ibexes with exaggerated horns and raised tails may indicate a sacred connection between ibex, psychoactive mushrooms growing on their dung, and human spiritual practices (Orrelle, 2022, 6–7). Mushroom symbolism permeates artifacts across the region, from pottery to monumental stone structures. This prevalence implies that entheogen use was deeply integrated into the culture, persisting for millennia before Sumerian times.

As we examine Sumerian culture and the legends of the Anunnaki, we must consider how this older tradition of altered consciousness may have shaped their beliefs and practices. The mushroom cult of the Southern Levant invites a reevaluation of the roots of Near Eastern spirituality and the possible entheogenic foundations of early civilizations. Sumerian priests and wise men actively sought out these and other psychoactive plants, incorporating them into religious ceremonies and using them as tools for divination. In this view, the altered states achieved through these substances were not seen as separate from reality, but as a means of accessing a higher truth, of communing directly with the gods. The knowledge imparted by the Anunnaki was not limited to practical skills like agriculture and metallurgy but extended to the mysteries of the cosmos and the nature of the soul. There is archaeological evidence that suggest that the Anunnaki may have imparted knowledge of mind-altering substances to humanity as a means of accessing higher states of consciousness.

Ancient astronauts shaping the cradle of civilization, divine rulers wielding unfathomable power over mortal affairs, the lone technocratic elite survivors of a pre-flood cataclysm: The most powerful entities of humanity's oldest myths and legends have worn many masks. The question persists: Who or *what* are the Anunnaki? You can look for the answers in the mainstream academic corpus, but now, even once daring speculations and theories that sought to challenge conventional narratives have become mainstream. In fact, they have become so mainstream, that theories about the Anunnaki are now a big part of the pop-cultural milieu. This polarization has most people trapped between a stagnant elitist academic explanation for these ancient mysteries and a growing cottage industry of influencers who peddle the Anunnaki as clickbait mixing half-truths, luxury branding, and spiritual jargon into a product designed to capitalize, not illuminate.

The Mesopotamian stories of the Anunnaki bringing civilization to humanity may represent more than myth. Interpreted symbolically, these figures embody a deeper pattern: the emergence of higher states of awareness through altered states of consciousness. Rather than literal gods descending from the sky, they may reflect visionary encounters accessible through shamanic experience and ritual use of psychoactive substances (Strassman, 2001). In the chapters ahead, I will examine artifacts that have been either dismissed by scholars or distorted by popular media. These include the so-called handbags of the gods and the Anunnaki wristwatches, recurring symbols found not only in Mesopotamian art but across geographically and temporally distant cultures. Their persistence suggests the existence of a shared symbolic lexicon rooted in the cognitive architecture of the human mind.

The Anunnaki are not the only figures described in these texts. There are also the Apkallu, beings who bridge the human and the divine. According to the Sumerians, these sages walked among kings, transmitted sacred knowledge, and guided humanity through periods of chaos and regeneration. They do not resemble aliens in the cinematic sense. They are portrayed as intermediaries, half-immortal agents of order, wisdom, and encoded memory. To understand what these figures truly represent, I had to move beyond abstract interpretation. Their meaning is not confined to dusty texts or speculative theories. It is embedded in carved stone and symbolic motifs they left behind. These artifacts are not just remnants of a forgotten past. They are instruments of initiation. I needed to see them for myself.

CHAPTER 3

THE CULT OF THE POPPY

Hul Gil Rite, Wristwatches, and Handbags of the Gods

Opium teaches only one thing, which is that aside from physical suffering, there is nothing real.

—ANDRÉ MALRAUX

Gods, Aliens, Angels, or Demons?

As my research progressed, I found myself standing in a hushed museum gallery, transfixed by the towering Assyrian relief before me. I was face to face with an Apkallu, one of a strange and mysterious group of seven wise humanoid beings believed to have come to Earth to teach humans the technologies of civilization. A text from Uruk lists the antediluvian kings and the seven antediluvian sages, each Apkallu associated with a particular role, such as fire, medicine, law, handcraft, and art. The Apkallu were often depicted as half-fish, half-human, or as people in fish costumes. Babylonian incantation texts describe the Apkallu in other forms as well. While the Apkallu were credited with helping humans build civilization, they were not always portrayed in a positive light. Some Mesopotamian tablets describe them more as demons or malevolent entities, likely because of their association with magic. In some texts, it is said that they rebelled against the gods, angering them, much like the original angels in Abrahamic beliefs. However, the exact nature of their transgression is unclear. The fragmentary texts do not fully explain how the Apkallu angered the primary gods.

Scholar Erica Reiner, an editor of the *Chicago Assyrian Dictionary (CAD)*, believed that Assyrian scribes deliberately suppressed parts of their most ancient history that might explain why these beings fell from grace. She theorized that they angered the gods through some form of hubris, what she termed an "excessive manifestation of their super-human capacity" (Reiner, 1961). These ancient and mysterious sages are among the oldest known descriptions of discarnate beings that intercede between humanity and an ultimate consciousness residing on a metaphysical plane of existence. Such an important historical and theological concept deserves more careful analysis but is routinely overlooked by mainstream scholars. What exactly were these beings? Why were they intentionally erased from the historical record? Are they still relevant today?

This raises further questions about the nature of these discarnate entities. Could angels and demons, as described in ancient religious texts, be the same as modern descriptions of extraterrestrials? The line between these beings is often thin, with entities like Lucifer being described as a fallen angel. As Abrahamic religions developed, many pagan deities were demonized, and the distinction between angels and demons became more pronounced. Could it be that these beings, whether seen as gods, angels, demons, or aliens, are manifestations of the same phenomenon viewed through different cultural lenses?

Our hyperconnected digital world has opened our eyes to our shared experiences, revealing that we are more alike than we once realized. We are similar to one another, and we can relate to the experiences of people in ancient civilizations. We are beginning to notice that something in these experiences is universal. Mainstream academicians have often rebuffed these universalities in favor of a deconstructed view of history. Postmodern philosophers have woven a thread of skepticism through universal or grand narratives, making it quite radical to suggest a continuity derived from something greater than ourselves. Such considerations are often dismissed as pseudoscience. As a historian of the human mind and cognitive archaeologist, I regularly sift through the ash heap of history, searching for clues to the mysteries deemed unsolvable. In doing so, I have found striking similarities between the myths of ancient discarnate entities and those of modern ones, like aliens. Could it be that these beings are manifestations of the same phenomenon, viewed through the lens of different cultures and times?

As I stood, lost in thought, before this Assyrian relief, I was reminded of what my old friend Whitley Strieber, author of *Communion,* once said: "Whatever the visitors are, I suspect they have been responsible for much paranormal phenomena, ranging from the appearance of gods, angels, fairies, ghosts and miraculous beings to the landing of UFOs in the backyards of America" (Strieber, 2011, ~43:00). The ancient carving seemed to take on new life and hidden meaning, its eyes holding secrets that had eluded scholars for generations. In that moment, I felt the first threads of a new mystery unraveling before me, one that would lead me down a path of discovery I could scarcely have imagined.

The masterfully crafted image seemed to come alive as I examined the rosette motifs that had puzzled scholars for generations. My eyes were drawn to the flowers held by the enigmatic genii figures, and suddenly, a jolt of recognition shot through me—these weren't just any flowers; they were *poppies*. The realization hit me with such force that I took an involuntary step back. My mind raced, connecting dots I'd been studying for years. Here, before my eyes, was evidence that these rosettes and plant images weren't mere decorative elements. They were a code, hidden in plain sight.

Assyrian relief of Saluting Protective Spirit (883–859 BCE) from Nimrud Northwest Palace, located at the Cleveland Museum of Art, Cleveland, OH

The prevalence of these poppy-like rosettes in Mesopotamian iconography wasn't just artistic convention, it was a visual key to understanding their rituals and beliefs. Standing there, lost in contemplation, I barely noticed the other museum-goers shuffling past. How many others had looked at this same relief, not realizing they were seeing a millennia-old testament to the use of psychoactive substances in religious and royal rituals?

I reached for my notebook, eager to capture this revelation before it could slip away. The connection between these ancient symbols and the psychoactive properties of the opium poppy offered a new lens through which to view Assyrian art and religion. I sketched the rosette patterns in my notebook while my mind wandered to the broader implications of this discovery.

As these designs grew increasingly stylized over time, they likely developed into a codified visual language representing altered states of consciousness and divine revelation. The persistent association of these floral motifs with supernatural beings like genii or Apkallu underscores their role in bridging mortal and divine realms. These entities, often depicted with distinctive rosette "wristwatches" reminiscent of poppy capsules, can be interpreted as guides facilitating transcendent experiences through entheogenic substances. A careful examination of these individual symbols: the rosettes, pinecones, the so-called wristwatches and handbags, and the Sumerian votive statuettes, may help us solve this ancient mystery.

Rosettes

Rosettes were among the most common and widely discussed ornamental motifs in ancient Near Eastern art. Helen J. Kantor, a renowned scholar of ancient Near Eastern art, provides a succinct definition: "Rosettes are among the most commonly found and most widely discussed ornamental motives. The term, which can be used to cover all radially symmetrical circular designs (all the radial elements of which are frequently identical in form), is usually considered to denote decorations derived from plant forms" (Kantor, 1947). This definition highlights the ubiquity of rosettes in ancient Near Eastern iconography and their likely origin in natural forms, particularly flowers.

The prevalence of rosettes in Mesopotamian iconography suggests a deep cultural significance, one that likely extended beyond mere decorative appeal. Their radial symmetry and floral associations made them ideal symbols for celestial bodies, divine emanation, and the cyclical nature of life and death, all concepts central to Mesopotamian cosmology and religion. Evidence for opium poppy cultivation and use in Mesopotamia dates back to at least the third millennium BCE.

While cannabis was also cultivated early in human history, particularly in Central Asia and China, the opium poppy appears to have held special significance in the Near East. Mark D. Merlin, an expert on the history of psychoactive plant use, notes that the earliest human use of cannabis appears to have occurred in the steppe regions of Central Asia or in China (2003). Hemp was certainly one of the earliest crop plants of China. Over hundreds, perhaps thousands of years, early inhabitants of Central and/or Eastern Asia domesticated cannabis varieties from wild plants into artificially selected, cultivated crops (Merlin, 2003). This observation, while focusing on cannabis, underscores the ancient relationship between humans and psychoactive plants, a relationship that would have included the opium poppy in Mesopotamia.

The earliest known Egyptian rosettes provide intriguing evidence of Mesopotamian influence and the early significance of this motif. Merlin observes: "The earliest Egyptian rosettes known are incised or carved on gold and ivory knife handles of the late Gerzean phase, where they serve as filling motives for the design of intertwined snakes that is among the antithetical motives introduced at this time by Mesopotamian influence" (Merlin, 2003, 300). This early connection between rosette designs and Mesopotamian culture hints at the motif's importance in the region and its potential association with sacred or magical practices.

Pinecones

The pinecone, with its numerous seeds and symmetrical form, has long been associated with fertility, regeneration, and enlightenment across various cultures. In Assyrian iconography, it often appears in the hands of divine or semidivine figures, seemingly used in a gesture of blessing or purification. The pine tree, from which the cone comes, specifically the Turkish Pine, or *Pinus brutia*, was known in the region for its longevity and evergreen nature, making it a potent symbol of immortality and divine knowledge.

The juxtaposition of poppy-derived imagery with pinecones in Assyrian scenes is particularly telling. While the rosette motif symbolizes the psychoactive agent, the pinecone likely represents the act of imparting divine wisdom or initiating the subject into sacred mysteries. This dual symbolism creates a rich visual metaphor for the process of achieving enlightenment through altered states of consciousness. As I continued my examination of the relief, the scenes depicting genii anointing kings with pinecones took on new significance. These could be viewed as symbolic representations of royal initiation rites involving the use of psychoactive substances to access divine knowledge. Such practices would have been crucial for righteous and divinely guided rule, embedding the use of entheogens into the fabric of Assyrian political and religious life.

Relief of Apkallu holding a pinecone

When combined with the rosette motif, likely representing the opium poppy, the pinecone creates a powerful symbolic dyad. The rosette, embodying the means of altering consciousness, pairs with the pinecone, representing the wisdom or divine insight gained through that altered state. This combination suggests a sophisticated understanding of entheogenic practices, where the use of psychoactive substances was seen not as an end in itself, but as a tool for accessing higher realms of knowledge and spirituality. The pinecone was also associated with the pineal gland, sometimes referred to as the third eye in esoteric traditions. The pineal gland produces melatonin, a hormone that regulates sleep patterns and is thought to produce trace amounts of dimethyltryptamine (DMT), a powerful psychedelic compound.

The gesture of anointing with a pinecone could thus be interpreted as a symbolic activation of this third eye. When considered alongside the rosette symbolism, it suggests a sophisticated understanding of altered states of consciousness and the means to induce them. The pinecone might represent the innate human capacity for transcendent experiences, while the rosette symbolizes the external catalyst (opium) that activates this capacity. This dual symbolism of internal capacity (pinecone/pineal gland) and external catalyst (rosette/opium) mirrors modern understandings of psychedelic experiences as an interaction between the substance ingested and the individual's mind. It suggests that the Assyrians may have had a nuanced understanding of the interplay between brain chemistry and external substances in producing altered states of consciousness. Scenes depicting genii anointing kings with pinecones take on new significance in this context. These can be viewed as symbolic representations of royal initiation rites involving the use of psychoactive substances to access divine knowledge. Such practices would have been crucial for righteous and divinely guided rule, embedding the use of entheogens into the fabric of Assyrian political and religious life.

The act of anointing, a practice found in many ancient cultures, was traditionally seen as a way of conferring divine favor or marking someone for a sacred purpose. In the Assyrian context, the use of the pinecone for this act, combined with the presence of rosette motifs, implies a ritual that went beyond mere symbolism. It suggests a practice where the king, through the intercession of the Apkallu and the use of psychoactive substances (represented by the rosette), was brought into direct communion with the divine.

This interpretation aligns with what we know of ancient Near Eastern concepts of kingship. The king was often viewed as a mediator between the gods and humans, responsible for maintaining cosmic order. His ability to commune directly with the gods would have been seen as essential for this role. The use of entheogens in this context would have been viewed not as a recreational activity, but as a solemn and necessary duty, crucial for the well-being of the entire kingdom. The consistent appearance of the pinecone motif across centuries of Assyrian art implies a long-standing tradition of entheogen use deeply woven into the culture's spiritual and political practices. This enduring symbolism points to the central role that altered states of consciousness, achieved through the use of substances like opium, played in Assyrian concepts of divine kingship and cosmic order. The fact that the simple, undivided rosette was not typically used in architectural decoration implies that its use was reserved for more intimate or sacred contexts, perhaps those associated with ritual or royal regalia. Archaeological evidence proves this connection without a doubt, as the anointing scenes, along with rosettes, can be found on the royal jewelry that was excavated from The Queen's Tombs at Nimrud in what is now modern-day Mosul, Iraq.

The Anunnaki Gold, Wristwatches, and the Legacy of Muzahim Hussein

In 1989, Muzahim Mahmoud Hussein, an esteemed Iraqi archaeologist, made a groundbreaking discovery at Nimrud, unearthing the Queens' Tombs beneath the Northwest Palace of King Ashurnasirpal II. This find would later be recognized as one of the most significant archaeological discoveries of the twentieth century, shedding light on the burial practices, wealth, and spirituality of the Neo-Assyrian elite. Within these tombs were treasures beyond imagination—crowns, jewelry, and ceremonial objects—that spoke to the opulence and sacred rites of Assyria's royal women. Among these treasures, certain artifacts hinted at deeper, mystical practices, possibly linked to what I call the Hul Gil Rite, an ancient ceremonial use of the opium poppy.

The contents of the Queens' Tombs were astonishing, even by the standards of previous Assyrian finds. Hussein's excavation revealed four intact burial chambers, each containing the remains of queens adorned with intricate golden jewelry, inlaid with semi-precious stones like lapis lazuli, agate, and carnelian. Among the most remarkable pieces was a gold crown weighing over a kilogram, found on the head of one queen. The crown, adorned with 140 delicate grape leaves and clusters of lapis lazuli grapes, was held up by eight winged female genii, symbols of divine protection. But it was the lower half of the crown that captured the greatest attention—three rows of opium poppy capsules alternated with granulated rosettes, hinting at a sacred symbolism (Hussein, 2016).

Initially, these poppy capsules were mistaken for pomegranates by some scholars, including Dominique Collon (2008, 106). However, Hussein later corrected this assumption, identifying them as opium poppy capsules. Interestingly, earlier works by local researchers had already recognized them as poppy capsules and flowers, but the interpretation shifted, perhaps due to changing cultural attitudes, such as the global war on drugs (Hussein, 2016). This discovery sheds light on the role the poppy played in Assyrian burial rites, perhaps not merely as a decorative motif but as a plant imbued with religious and ritual significance. The idea that the queens may have used opium as part of their spiritual practices—either in life or in the afterlife—adds a fascinating layer to our understanding of Assyrian royal customs.

Alongside the crown, Hussein unearthed an array of bracelets and armlets, some of which have been described in pseudoarchaeological circles as *wristwatches of the gods*. These objects, with their concentric designs and inlaid stones, were found on the wrists of several queens. Rather than dismissing these interpretations outright, it's worth considering that these artifacts carried significant symbolic meaning. The intricate designs, featuring genii, rosettes, and the tree of life, evoke themes of protection, renewal, and divine favor (Hussein, 2016). Whether or not these items had a practical or technological function beyond their ceremonial use, their presence in the tombs underscores their importance in Assyrian royal culture.

The gold bracelets discovered in Tomb II, for example, were adorned with scenes of kneeling genii holding pinecones and buckets—a common motif symbolizing fertility and protection. Other bracelets featured pairs of lion heads with turquoise inlays for eyes, while some displayed rosettes surrounding a central eye stone. These motifs, long associated with Neo-Assyrian religious iconography, might have served to protect the wearer both in life and death, connecting the queens to divine forces. The symbolic connection between these pieces and the opium poppy suggests that the queens may have been participants in the Hul Gil Rite, communing with the divine through the use of opium to achieve altered states of consciousness (Hussein, 2016).

Muzahim Hussein's careful excavation and documentation of these treasures were a monumental achievement, but they were also nearly lost forever. Following the 2003 invasion of Iraq, the Iraq National Museum and its associated institutions, including the State Board of Antiquities and Heritage (SBAH), were looted, and thousands of priceless artifacts were stolen or destroyed. Hussein's discovery, which had been housed in the museum's storerooms, was no exception. The looters, indifferent to the cultural and historical value of the artifacts, ransacked the museum, leaving behind only chaos. Many of the records associated with Hussein's work were either destroyed or scattered, and the gold from the tombs was nearly lost in the vaults of Baghdad's Central Bank, which was bombed during the conflict (Hussein, 2016). Remarkably, some of the objects were recovered after months of effort, thanks in part to the dedication of Hussein and his colleagues.

The looting of Iraq's cultural heritage was a profound tragedy, and for scholars like Hussein, it was deeply personal. Eighty years of archaeological records, manuscripts, and photographs were lost or damaged, including those documenting Hussein's work at Nimrud. Despite these setbacks, Hussein's contributions remain invaluable. His meticulous attention to detail, particularly in recognizing the significance of the poppy imagery on the Queens' regalia, has opened new avenues for understanding Mesopotamian spiritual practices.

In *Nimrud: The Queens' Tombs*, a collaboration between Hussein, Mark Altaweel, and McGuire Gibson, the legacy of this discovery is preserved. The book provides a detailed account of the treasures found within the tombs and the context in which they were unearthed. It also serves as a record of the poppy's symbolic importance, emphasizing its potential role in royal Assyrian rituals. Whether used in life or prepared for use in the afterlife, the opium poppy, or *Hul Gil* as it was known, played a vital role in these ancient rites (Hussein, 2016).

The so-called wristwatches found on the queens are not mere trinkets but deeply symbolic objects, possibly connected to the Hul Gil Rite, or Opium Poppy Rite. As the queens were interred with these ceremonial items, adorned with motifs of divine genii and sacred plants, it is plausible to imagine that they believed in the poppy's ability to open the door to the divine, guiding them through death into the next realm (Hussein, 2016).

"Wristwatch of the Gods"—Gold Bracelet for the Treasures Found in Royal Tomb. Depicts poppy flowers and the Apkallu performing the Hu Gil Rite.

With my notebook filled with sketches and observations, I finally stepped away from the relief, unable to shake the feeling that I had stumbled upon something profound. I remembered an old book I had in my library at home; it showed these wristwatches in great detail, and one in particular that was found during an excavation in beautiful condition. The Assyrian artifacts around me were no longer just relics of a long-gone civilization; they were keys to understanding a complex system of belief and practice, one that might offer insights into the very nature of human consciousness and our quest for transcendence.

The implications of this discovery stretched far beyond the walls of the museum. It challenged not only our understanding of ancient Mesopotamian cultures but also our modern conceptions of consciousness, spirituality, and the potential of the human mind. As I made my way out of the gallery, my mind buzzed with questions and possibilities. What other secrets might be hiding in plain sight, waiting for us to view them through the right lens?

The wristwatch of the gods motif, featuring a rosette bracelet worn by winged genii or Apkallu, may very well represent a stylized top view of a poppy seed capsule. This interpretation gains further credence when we consider the ancient techniques of harvesting poppies, particularly in Mesopotamia. Poppy harvesting, an ancient practice, involves making small incisions in the unripe seed capsules of the poppy plant, allowing the latex to ooze out and dry before collecting it. This latex is the source of opium, a substance that held significant ritual and medicinal value in the ancient world. The incision is typically made in a circular pattern around the capsule, and as the latex dries, it takes on a distinctive, star-shaped appearance. This process may have inspired the design of the rosette bracelet, symbolizing not just the poppy itself, but also its potent effects and its connection to divine or shamanic experiences.

To illustrate this, we can look at a detailed botany print of the poppy plant, which shows the seed capsule in its full form. The top view of the capsule, with its radiating lines, bears a striking resemblance to the rosette motif seen on the bracelets. This connection is not merely coincidental; rather, it suggests a deliberate choice by the artisans and priests to link the physical properties of the poppy with its symbolic and ritualistic significance.

Next, we turn to the wristwatch, or more aptly, bracelet. The image clearly shows the intricate design, with each "petal" of the rosette resembling the dried latex patterns on a poppy capsule. This stylistic choice reinforces the idea that the bracelet was not just ornamental but held deeper meanings tied to the cultivation and use of the poppy in ancient rituals. By analyzing the bracelet in this context, we see how the motif serves as a visual metaphor, connecting the wearer to the divine properties of the poppy. This connection likely extended beyond mere decoration,

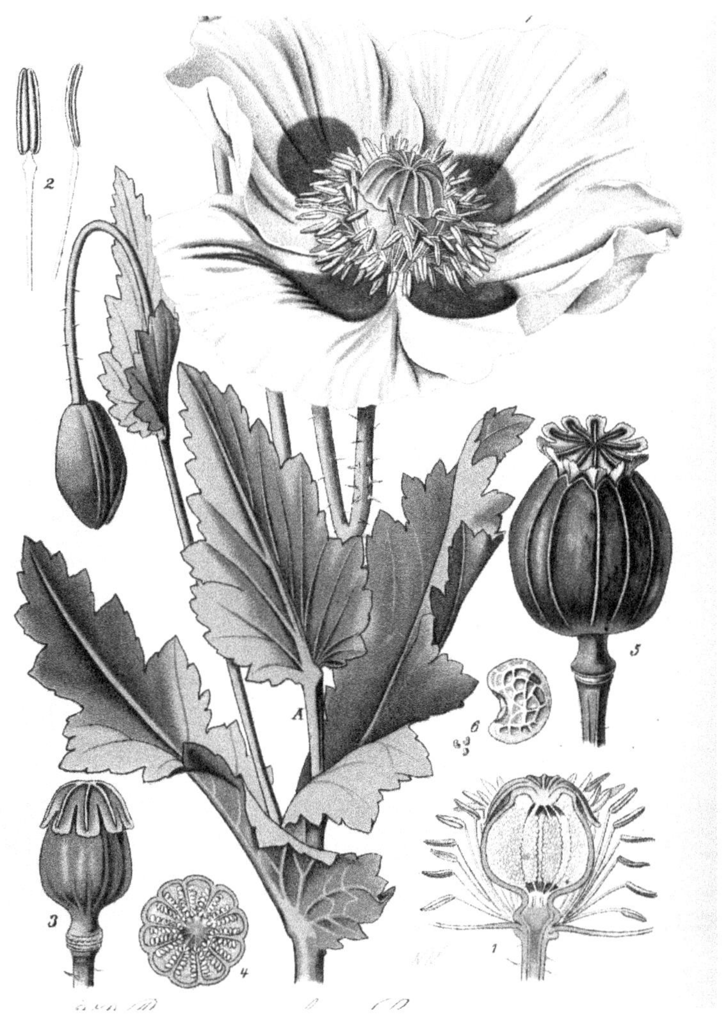

Illustration of Papaver somniferum. *A botanical illustration of the opium poppy, which has been historically significant in various cultures for its medicinal and psychoactive properties.*

embodying the belief that the poppy, and by extension the bracelet, held the power to bridge the human and divine, possibly even aiding in communication with the gods or in accessing altered states of consciousness. The Apkallu, often depicted in acts of anointment or blessing, may have been seen as intermediaries capable of inducing or guiding transcendent experiences. This distinctive motif, where the rosette appears as a bracelet or wrist ornament on divine figures, is particularly intriguing. In many cultures, wrists are considered spiritually significant points on the body, associated with pulse, life force, and the flow of energy. The placement of the rosette at this point on the body of divine beings could symbolize their control over life forces, their ability to manipulate consciousness, or their role as dispensers of divine wisdom. They are always depicted on the left hand, perhaps linking to the heart. Additionally, the circular shape of the rosette, when worn as a bracelet, creates a visual link to the cycle of time and the eternal nature of the divine. It may have represented the gods' mastery over time and their ability to grant visions of past, present, and future to those who partook in sacred rituals involving entheogens.

Handbags

The internet brims with images of these mysterious handbags and the modern tools carried by astronauts. While humorous, these memes symbolize humanity's enduring quest to traverse and understand the celestial. Such comparisons evoke images of ancient deities carrying tokens of cosmic origin, wrapping the ancient and modern in a shared narrative of celestial exploration and reverence.

The term *handbags of the gods* was coined by author Zecharia Sitchin, who first noted the peculiar presence of bag-like objects in the hands of divine figures in ancient Sumerian and Mesopotamian art (Sitchin, 1976). These handbags, often held by deities or mythical heroes, appear in various forms, from simple pouches to ornate, decorative satchels. What are these objects and could they have held sacred objects, powerful talismans, or even advanced technological devices?

Similar depictions of handbags can be found in ancient Egyptian art, where deities like Osiris and Isis are often portrayed holding ankh symbols and small bags (Wilkinson, 2003). These bags, known as *sa*, were believed to contain magical or divine objects that granted the gods their power and authority. Intriguingly, the handbag motif is not limited to the ancient Near East

Stone relief, North-West Palace, Nimrud, Iraq, ninth century BCE. Detailed relief of the hand of an Apkallu, a protective spirit, wearing a bracelet and holding a bucket for religious rituals.

and Egypt. In the ancient Andean civilizations of South America, figures holding bag-like objects can be found in various artistic representations (Stone-Miller, 2002). The Inca god Viracocha is often depicted holding a small bag, which some researchers believe may have contained sacred coca leaves or other ceremonial items, and a stone stele was found at the archeological site of La Venta, depicting the ancient Mesoamerican god Quetzalcoatl, holding in his hand a bag similar to the one we see in ancient Sumerian depictions.

The presence of these handbags across such diverse and geographically distant cultures has led to numerous theories and speculations about their true nature and purpose. Some researchers, like Sitchin, have suggested that the bags may have contained advanced technological devices or even nuclear weapons, pointing to the immense power and influence wielded by the gods who carried them (Sitchin, 1976). Others have proposed more mundane explanations, arguing that the handbags may have simply held everyday items of value, such as seeds, herbs, or precious stones. Still, the consistent association of these bags with divine or mythical figures suggests a deeper, more mysterious significance.

One of the most intriguing clues could come from the ancient Iranian plateau, where recent discoveries in the Jiroft region have shed new light on the iconography of divine handbags. The Jiroft civilization, which flourished in the late third millennium BCE, left behind a treasure trove of intricately carved objects made of chlorite—a group of phyllosilicate minerals that are a part of the mica group, typically greenish due to their iron and magnesium content, and indicative of low- to moderate-grade metamorphic processes.

These chlorite artifacts, including vessels, ceremonial weights, and the so-called handbags (Perrot and Majidzadeh, 2005), were adorned with iconography depicting animals, mythical creatures, and geometric patterns and provide a possible glimpse into the beliefs and cosmology of this forgotten culture. The Jiroft civilization, which flourished in the late third millennium BCE in what is now the Sistan, Baluchestan, and Kerman provinces of Iran, represents a significant, yet often overlooked, chapter in the history of ancient Near Eastern cultures. Recent discoveries at sites such as Konar Sandal, Shahr-e Sukhteh, and Tepe Yahya have revealed a complex society that may have served as an intermediary between the well-known civilizations of Elam to the west and the Indus Valley to the east. This strategic position likely enabled the Jiroft culture to develop a unique intercultural style, reflected in the artifacts unearthed in this region (Majidzadeh, 2003).

Motifs, such as the handbags, suggest a complex cosmology where the natural and supernatural realms intersect, and where objects like these handbags played a critical role in mediating between the divine and the earthly (Perrot and Majidzadeh, 2008).

Artifact from the Jiroft culture in southeastern Iran

The chlorite artifacts from Jiroft are not merely decorative; they speak to the culture's connections with other ancient civilizations and hint at a possible exchange of ideas and beliefs. The unique "intercultural style" identified in these artifacts has led some scholars, such as Yusef Majidzadeh, to propose that Jiroft represented an independent Bronze Age civilization with its own distinct language and architectural style. However, this hypothesis remains debated, with some archaeologists like Oscar Muscarella urging caution and emphasizing the need for further scholarly publication and stratigraphic analysis to fully understand the site's significance (Muscarella, 2003).

Despite the ongoing debates, what is clear is that the Jiroft culture's artistic and ritualistic contributions are profound. The depiction of mythical creatures and geometric patterns on these objects reflects a worldview in which the boundaries between the mundane and the mystical were fluid (Lamberg-Karlovsky, 2003). Such a perspective aligns with the broader use of similar objects across ancient Near Eastern cultures where ritual implements often played a dual role as both functional and symbolic items, embodying the connection between humanity and the divine.

Chlorite, a soft, easily worked stone, was abundant in the mineral-rich region around Jiroft, which also boasted deposits of copper, gold, and even meteoritic iron (Kohl, 2009). Could it be that these handbags were more than just symbolic accessories and might have served as containers for sacred substances imbued with celestial power? The idea is not as far-fetched as it may seem. In Mesopotamian art, divine figures are often depicted holding a "purifier" (*mullilu*) in one hand and a "bucket" (*banduddû*) in the other (Wiggermann, 1992). These ritual implements were used in purification ceremonies, where the mullilu, a type of conifer cone, was dipped into the banduddû, which held sacred water or other holy liquids. The parallels to the Jiroft handbags are striking—both in form and potential function—but the connection goes deeper still. The iconography adorning the Jiroft artifacts hints at a complex cosmology where the natural and supernatural realms intersect. Hybrid creatures, part human and part animal, cavort alongside realistic depictions of local flora and fauna (Perrot and Majidzadeh, 2005). These images suggest a worldview in which the boundaries between the mundane and the mystical were fluid, where gods and mortals could commune through the medium of sacred objects and substances.

This idea of divine intermediaries is further reinforced by the depiction of "sages" or Apkallu in Assyrian art. These mythical beings, often shown with the heads of birds or other animals, served as conduits between the heavenly and earthly realms. Their association with the mullilu and banduddû suggests that these ritual implements were not mere tools, but rather powerful talismans that allowed the sages to bridge the gap between the gods and humanity (Black and Green, 1992). Intriguingly, the sages are sometimes depicted carrying handbags remarkably similar to those found at Jiroft and elsewhere in the ancient Near East. This further underscores the idea that these objects were not just symbolic accessories, but instead served a vital function in the religious and ritual practices of the time.

The discovery of chlorite objects in Jiroft, which may have been used to store meteoritic fragments, adds another layer to our understanding, potentially linking these handbags to celestial phenomena and reaffirming humanity's long-standing veneration of the stars (Kohl, 2009). Such objects were likely symbols of identity and status, with the act of carrying them signifying one's affiliation and role within the society's social and religious structure. The mythical creatures and abstract patterns that adorn these objects may not represent gods per se, but rather the forces of nature and the cosmos that humans could harness and control through the use of sacred substances and rituals (Eliade, 1964). This idea of human agency in the face of cosmic forces is a recurring theme in the iconography of ancient Iran. From the heroic exploits of legendary kings to the cosmic battles between good and evil that would later form the basis of Zoroastrian dualism, Iranian mythology is replete with stories of mortals who dared to challenge the gods and shape their own destinies (Kellens, 1989).

This perspective on the handbags as markers of identity is affirmed by their symbolic presence in global mythologies, from the medicine bags of Native American shamans to the treasure sacks of Chinese Daoist immortals (Eliade, 1964). The recurrent motif of sacred containers across civilizations suggests that the handbags were part of a broader lexicon of cultural and cosmological meanings, transcending their functional use to embody the spiritual aspirations and practices of ancient societies. What, then, are we to make of the Jiroft handbags and their Mesopotamian counterparts? Are they mere coincidences of form and function, or do they reflect a deeper pattern of cultural exchange and adaptation?

The answer, as with so much in the study of ancient iconography, is likely a bit of both. On one level, the similarities between the Jiroft and Mesopotamian handbags may simply reflect the practical needs of ritual and ceremony in the ancient world (Casanova, 1991). In a time before mass-produced containers and synthetic materials, the use of stone vessels and woven bags to hold sacred substances would have been a logical choice for religious practitioners and elites alike. On a deeper level, however, the recurrence of the handbag motif across time and space suggests that these objects tapped into something more fundamental in the human psyche—a desire to connect with the divine, to harness the power of the cosmos, and to assert one's place in the grand drama of existence (Eliade, 1964). The Jiroft handbags, with their exquisite craftsmanship and familiar iconography, offer a glimpse into this ancient and enduring fascination with the sacred and the supernatural.

Containers

Ancient Mesopotamians likely used specialized containers to collect opium latex from poppy plants. Archaeological evidence suggests the use of small vessels that would have been ideal for scraping the sticky latex from scored poppy pods. These containers, often adorned with poppy-inspired motifs, have been found at sites dating back to the third millennium BCE (Merlin, 2003). The effects of opium derived from poppies include pain relief, euphoria, and altered states of consciousness. These properties made it valuable for both medicinal and ritual purposes in ancient cultures. The ability of opium to induce vivid dreams and visions may have been particularly significant in religious contexts, possibly facilitating communication with deities or the spirit world (Rudgley, 1999).

Studies have found compelling evidence of opium residue in ancient artifacts, supporting theories about the use and trade of opium in antiquity. Zuzanna Chovanec and her colleagues discovered opium alkaloids in Bronze Age Cypriot base-ring juglets, providing chemical proof of opium's presence in these vessels (Chovanec et al., 2015). This finding not only confirms the use of opium in the ancient Mediterranean but also suggests a sophisticated understanding of the plant's properties and methods of extraction.

The Hul Gil Rite: An Ancient Sumerian Practice

The Hul Gil Rite, as I have termed it, was a sacred ritual practiced by the Sumerians, centered around the use of the opium poppy, a plant deeply embedded in their spiritual practices. The Hul Gil

Rite represents the practical method by which human Anunnaki shamans accessed the realm of the Apkallu. The human practitioners used opium and other consciousness-altering substances to commune with the discarnate teachers (Apkallu), who then imparted the knowledge that became the foundation of civilization. The term *Hul Gil* is derived from the Sumerian ideograms *Hul* and *Gil*, found on a clay tablet from Nippur dating back to the Third Dynasty of Ur (2100–2000 BCE) (Civil, 1960). These ideograms have been interpreted as referring to the opium poppy, often described as the "plant of joy," which was believed to have profound psychoactive and spiritual effects (Terry and Pellens, 1970). Roberta Dougherty of Yale University translated the basic meaning of *Hul* as "joy" or "rejoicing," while *Gil* represented various plants. When combined, these symbols may have depicted a plant capable of producing a sense of delight or satisfaction.

For decades, many scholars interpreted Hul Gil as referring to the opium poppy, leading to speculation about the use of opium in ancient Sumerian rituals. In the ritual, the Apkallu are shown anointing the king with a pinecone, symbolically opening his third eye to divine knowledge. This pinecone was likely dipped in a substance derived from the opium poppy and stored in a nonporous handbag, possibly similar to those found in Jiroft. The king, often depicted wearing cuffs that match those discovered in the Queen's tomb at Nimrud, would undergo a transformation, connecting with the divine to legitimize his rule and gain the wisdom necessary to govern.

This rite highlights the Sumerians' belief in the opium poppy's power to bridge the mortal and divine realms. Despite some scholarly debate over the interpretation of these ideograms and the extent of the poppy's use in Mesopotamian culture, the persistence of the idea that the poppy played a significant role in their religious practices remains compelling. Through the Hul Gil

Relief; Nimrud, Iraq, 865–60 BCE. This relief depicts the Assyrian king Ashurnasirpal II performing religious rituals before the sacred tree, symbolizing divine approval of his reign (Hul Gil Ritual?).

Rite, the king's spiritual and temporal authority was reinforced, ensuring his connection to the gods and his right to rule. Whether through pharmacological effects or the power of belief, this rite likely played a significant role in Sumerian religious and political life, setting a precedent for later Near Eastern practices involving sacred plants and anointing rituals.

Votives

The Sumerian votive statues, with their distinctive eyes, are often found in large numbers at excavation sites. They depict worshippers in various poses of devotion, frequently holding small vessels, presumably for ritual libations, and could offer additional evidence of potential entheogen use in one of the world's earliest civilizations. What makes these figures particularly intriguing is the distinct and varied representation of their eyes, especially the pupils, which may provide insight into the ritualistic use of psychoactive substances in Sumerian worship. Many of these votive statues are characterized by huge staring eyes with notable pupils. This exaggerated feature has long been interpreted as an artistic convention meant to convey religious awe or attentiveness to the divine. However, when viewed through the lens of entheogen use, these dilated pupils take on new significance. Pupil dilation,

Sumerian Statue from Tell Asmar, part of the Tell Asmar Hoard, dating back to the Early Dynastic period of Mesopotamia, around 2900–2350 BCE. These statues are believed to have been used for religious or devotional purposes. Note the large eyes and holding of vessels.

or mydriasis, is a well-known physiological response to various psychoactive substances, including opiates and certain hallucinogens (Schultes and Hofmann, 1979). Conversely, some statues display pinpoint pupils, another ocular state associated with specific psychoactive substances. Miosis, or pupil constriction, is a hallmark effect of opiate use. The presence of both dilated and constricted pupils among these votive figures suggests a range of altered states, possibly induced by different substances or varying doses of the same substance.

The expressions on these statues are often described as rapt or transcendent, with a fixed, otherworldly gaze that seems to look beyond the physical realm. This representation aligns well with accounts of entheogenic experiences, where individuals often report a sense of connection with the divine or transcendence of ordinary reality. The Sumerians, with their complex pantheon and rich spiritual traditions, may have sought such transcendent states as a means of communing with their gods.

The small vessels held by many of these figures provide another clue to potential entheogen use. These containers, often cupped in the hands close to the body in a gesture of reverence, could have held ritual drinks infused with psychoactive substances. The act of drinking as part of religious ceremony is well-documented across many ancient cultures, from the *soma* of the Vedic tradition to the *kykeon* of the Eleusinian Mysteries (Wasson et al., 1978). The use of psychoactive substances in Mesopotamia bears intriguing parallels to practices in other ancient cultures. In Egypt, for instance, the blue lotus (*Nymphaea caerulea*) was used in religious contexts and depicted in art, suggesting a similar reverence for consciousness-altering plants (Emboden, 1981). In ancient Greece, the Eleusinian Mysteries involved the use of a mysterious substance, possibly ergot-derived, that induced profound mystical experiences (Wasson et al., 1978). These cross-cultural comparisons suggest a widespread human propensity for seeking altered states of consciousness, often within a spiritual or religious framework.

The sheer number of these votive statues found in Sumerian temples speaks to the widespread nature of these practices. If these figures do indeed represent worshippers in entheogen-induced altered states, it suggests that such experiences were not reserved for a select priesthood but were accessible to a broader segment of Sumerian society. This democratization of spiritual experience could have played a significant role in shaping Sumerian religious and social structures.

Cross-Cultural Early Evidence of Entheogen Use

The earliest-known Egyptian rosettes provide intriguing evidence of Mesopotamian influence and the early significance of this motif. Mark Merlin observes: "The earliest Egyptian rosettes known are incised or carved on gold and ivory knife handles of the late Gerzean phase, where they serve as filling motives for the design of intertwined snakes that is among the antithetical motives introduced at this time by Mesopotamian influence" (Merlin, 2003). This early connection between rosette designs and Mesopotamian culture hints at the motif's importance in the region and its potential association with sacred or magical practices.

This interpretation of Assyrian and Sumerian traditions aligns with other ancient cultures known to have used psychoactive substances in religious and royal contexts. The Indo-Iranian use of Soma suggests a broader ancient understanding of entheogens as tools for accessing divine realms and wisdom. *Soma* was a sacred drink mentioned in the *Rigveda*, an ancient Indian text, and in the *Avesta*, the primary collection of religious texts of Zoroastrianism.

The exact nature of soma has been debated by scholars for centuries, but many believe it was a preparation that included psychoactive plants (Furst, 1976). These practices appear to have been encoded in art for those initiated into their meaning.

In Vedic tradition, soma was personified as a god and was believed to grant divine inspiration, heroic strength, and even immortality. The preparation and consumption of soma was a central part of Vedic rituals, often associated with poetic inspiration and mystical insights. The parallels with the proposed Assyrian use of opium in royal and religious contexts are striking—in both cases, a plant-derived substance was seen as a means of bridging the gap between the human and divine realms.

As previously mentioned, the use of kykeon in Greek mystery cults, particularly in the Eleusinian Mysteries, offers another comparative point. Kykeon was a drink consumed as part of these mysteries, and while its exact composition is unknown, some scholars have suggested it may have contained psychoactive ingredients. The most prominent theory, proposed by R. Gordon Wasson, Albert Hofmann, and Carl A. P. Ruck in their book *The Road to Eleusis*, suggests that the kykeon may have contained ergot, a fungus that grows on rye and contains compounds similar to LSD (Wasson et al., 1978). The Eleusinian Mysteries were initiation ceremonies held every year for the cult of Demeter and Persephone in Eleusis, near Athens. These mysteries were among the most sacred and important religious rites of ancient Greece. They, like the proposed Assyrian practices, involved a ritual ingestion of a potentially psychoactive substance as part of a sacred ceremony. Participants reported profound mystical experiences and insights, which were considered so important and transformative that the details of the mysteries were kept secret on pain of death.

In Mesoamerica, we find another parallel in the use of psychoactive substances for religious and political purposes. The Aztec god Quetzalcoatl was said to have given humans sacred mushrooms, which were viewed as a source of wisdom and divine communication. The use of these mushrooms, along with other psychoactive plants like peyote, played a significant role in Mesoamerican religious practices and concepts of divine kingship (Furst, 1972).

While some have argued that empirical evidence for the deliberate induction of such states in Sumerian rituals remains elusive, the vivid and often surreal nature of their mythology has led others to posit the influence of non-ordinary conscious experiences on their spiritual cosmology. The Sumerian conception of the cosmos, populated by deities intimately involved in mortal affairs, suggests a perception of reality that transcends the mundane. Their mythological accounts, replete with descriptions of divine encounters and otherworldly journeys, bear striking parallels to phenomenological reports associated with altered states of consciousness. This correlation invites a reevaluation of Sumerian spiritual texts not merely as allegorical constructs, but as potential documentations of profound psychospiritual experiences.

The Sumerian cosmos was conceptualized as a dynamic, multilayered realm populated by a diverse pantheon of deities, each associated with various aspects of the natural world and human experience. The interactions between divine and mortal beings, as chronicled in Sumerian myths and religious texts, often exhibit characteristics that contemporary readers might categorize as oneiric or hallucinatory in nature. Consider, for instance, the *Epic of Gilgamesh*, one of the earliest extant works of literature. This story contains richly detailed descriptions of otherworldly peregrinations, encounters with chimerical entities, and direct communications with divine beings. While these elements are susceptible to purely allegorical or imaginative interpretations, some researchers have proposed that they might reflect experiential phenomena induced by altered states of consciousness, whether achieved through meditative practices, sensory deprivation techniques, or the ingestion of psychoactive compounds.

The concept of divine kingship, a cornerstone of Sumerian political and religious ideology, presents another intriguing avenue for exploration. Sumerian monarchs were perceived as divinely appointed, serving as intercessors between the celestial and terrestrial realms. This role necessitated a profound spiritual connection, often manifested through elaborate rituals and ceremonies. It is conceivable that these rites may have incorporated methodologies or substances designed to induce altered states, thereby facilitating a more direct communion with the divine. Sumerian religious architecture, particularly the imposing ziggurats that dominated their urban landscapes, points to the nature of their spiritual practices. These massive stepped structures, conceptualized as the earthly abodes of the gods, were loci of complex ritualistic activities. The ascent to the summit of a ziggurat, where the most sacred ceremonies were performed, could be interpreted as a physical manifestation of a spiritual journey, potentially mirroring an inner, psychospiritual ascent facilitated by altered states of consciousness.

We must remain cognizant of the inherent complexities and nuances of Sumerian spirituality, recognizing that it likely encompassed a wide spectrum of practices and experiences. This theory casts Sumerian spiritual leaders in a new light—not just as interpreters of divine will, but as psychonauts. They would have been responsible for not only administering these powerful substances but also for interpreting and integrating the resulting experiences into the broader cultural and religious framework. This suggests a "secret language" within religious texts. Similar theories have been proposed about various mystical traditions throughout history. If true in the Sumerian context, it would indicate a level of linguistic sophistication and intentional obfuscation that adds new depth to our understanding of this ancient culture.

According to Allegro (1970), this hidden language served a dual purpose: preserving sacred knowledge while also protecting it from misuse or persecution. The initiated would be able to discuss their entheogenic practices and experiences openly, yet opaquely, weaving a rich tapestry of allegory and metaphor that outsiders would interpret as standard religious discourse. The imagery of divine food or drink granting wisdom or immortality, common in many mythologies but particularly vivid in Sumerian tales, takes on new significance when viewed through this lens. Could the famous plant that granted immortality to Gilgamesh, only to be stolen by a serpent, be a reference to the *Amanita muscaria*?

Such interpretations invite us to reconsider the entire corpus of Sumerian mythology. Furthermore, Allegro proposes that this mushroom cult was not confined to Sumer alone. He suggests that it spread to other Mesopotamian cultures, influencing their religious practices and beliefs. This theory, if correct, would have far-reaching implications for our understanding of the development of religion in the ancient Near East and beyond. It raises the possibility that the use of entheogens played a crucial, yet hidden, role in shaping the spiritual landscape of multiple civilizations.

In Allegro's interpretation, certain Sumerian phrases and names serve as coded references to the preparation and use of psychoactive substances in rituals. This extends the impact of the proposed mushroom cult beyond the realm of personal spiritual experience and into the domain of formal religious practice. It suggests a systematic integration of entheogen use into the ritual life of Sumerian society, with carefully guarded knowledge passed down through generations of priests and initiates. While Allegro's theories remain controversial and are not widely accepted in mainstream academia, they offer an alternative perspective on Sumerian culture and religion—that one of the world's earliest civilizations was built on a foundation of entheogen-induced spiritual experiences. This view challenges our conventional understanding of the development of religion and society, suggesting that altered states of consciousness may have played a much more significant role in human cultural evolution than previously thought.

Whether one accepts Allegro's theories or not, they serve as a reminder of the complex and often surprising nature of ancient cultures. They encourage us to approach the study of these civilizations with open minds, ready to consider unconventional interpretations that might shed new light on age-old questions. In doing so, we may find that the ancient Sumerians, across the vast gulf of time, still have much to teach us about the nature of consciousness, spirituality, and the human quest for transcendence.

Beyond the Myths

Back in my study, I revisited the ancient texts with fresh eyes. The *Enuma Elish*, the Babylonian creation myth, now read like a metaphor for the battle between ordinary consciousness and the transcendental states accessed through psychedelics. Marduk's victory over Tiamat and the creation of the world from her body could symbolize the emergence of structured, dualistic reality from the undifferentiated unity of a psychedelic experience. The "gifts" of the Anunnaki—such as writing, mathematics, agriculture, and so on—might represent the insights gained through these experiences, insights that were then translated into the innovations that shaped human civilization.

The more I explored these connections, the more I realized that the Anunnaki myths were not just stories of gods and mortals—they were maps of consciousness, charting the territories of mind and spirit that humanity has explored for millennia. The recurring themes of divine beings imparting knowledge, the use of sacred plants, and the transformation of consciousness echoed across cultures and epochs, suggesting a shared, universal experience encoded in myth and ritual. Even Nibiru, that fabled celestial body often cited as the Anunnaki home world, takes on new meaning when viewed through this kaleidoscopic lens. Perhaps it's not a planet at all, but a state of consciousness, a phase in the cyclical evolution of human awareness that aligns with both ancient Mesopotamian cosmology and cutting-edge theories of consciousness. We will return to the Nibiru question in Chapter 5 where we will see that the Sumerians, like most ancient civilizations, had far greater knowledge of the cosmos than modern scholars acknowledge.

The mysteries of the Apkallu and their symbols, etched in stone, offer more than just a glimpse into Mesopotamian traditions. These ancient motifs and rituals carry echoes of a wisdom that transcended time and geography, leaving subtle imprints on civilizations around the world. The sacred objects and practices weren't merely relics; they were breadcrumbs meant to lead us down a path of esoteric knowledge, connecting cultures as diverse as ancient Egypt, Mesoamerica, and even the legends of lost civilizations like Atlantis. This encoded wisdom, preserved and transformed over millennia, suggests that the Anunnaki's influence may have reached further and deeper than we've ever imagined. The revelation awaits, and it is not limited to distant stars or ancient ruins, but extending beyond, into the unexplored frontiers of human consciousness.

CHAPTER 4

THE HIDDEN HISTORY OF HUMANITY

Younger Dryas and Ancient DNA Evidence

What we call the beginning is often the end.
And to make an end is to make a beginning.
The end is where we start from.

—T. S. ELIOT

In the last decade, a surge in discoveries about human evolution and the interplay between modern humans and archaic species like Neanderthals and Denisovans has reshaped our understanding of our ancient past. Central to these revelations is the work of geneticist David Reich at Harvard University, whose research has unveiled new dimensions of human ancestry (Reich, 2010). What was once considered a clean evolutionary tree—where modern

Homo sapiens stood alone—has now grown into a tangled web, with branches from archaic humans grafted onto the genomes of modern populations.

Reich's research has focused heavily on archaic humans, particularly Neanderthals, Denisovans, and other, yet-to-be-discovered species that may have contributed to our genetic makeup. In his lab, teams have sequenced the genomes of both modern humans and these archaic cousins, revealing a startling fact: Our DNA is a palimpsest. One of the most intriguing revelations involves the presence of *ghost DNA*, genetic material from extinct populations with no known fossil record. This ghost genetic contribution suggests that humans interbred with species beyond Neanderthals and Denisovans—ancient populations we have yet to fully identify (Reich, 2010). In this way, modern humans are connected not only to known species but also to these hidden branches of our evolutionary history, raising fundamental questions about what it means to be "modern."

The discovery of Denisovans was particularly shocking. Initially, all that was found was a finger bone in a Siberian cave—hardly enough evidence to suggest a new group of humans. But the DNA within that bone told a different story. It revealed an entirely separate lineage, distinct from Neanderthals but as genetically intertwined with modern humans as their Western Eurasian cousins (Reich, 2018). As more ancient DNA has been extracted, the lines between modern and archaic have blurred. The simple narrative of *Homo sapiens* as the pinnacle of human evolution has become an increasingly complex and interwoven tale of survival, adaptation, and genetic exchange.

This genetic mixing wasn't limited to ancient times. While the earliest interbreeding between modern humans and Neanderthals likely occurred sixty thousand to seventy thousand years ago, newer findings suggest multiple waves of gene flow, stretching much further into our evolutionary past. Mitochondrial DNA and Y-chromosome studies indicate that the last common maternal and paternal ancestors of Neanderthals and modern humans lived only three hundred thousand to four hundred thousand years ago—far more recently than the genomic data had previously suggested. In other words, some of the DNA that helps us trace our family lines back through generations may come not just from *Homo sapiens* but from these encounters with archaic human groups, including those only hinted at through ghost DNA (Reich, 2018).

Even the assumption that Neanderthals were a "sister species" to modern humans is being questioned. Some models suggest that up to 50 percent of Neanderthal DNA could have come from interactions with modern humans, meaning that Neanderthals might have absorbed large amounts of *Homo sapiens'* genes long before the two species officially diverged. This notion challenges the classic tree-of-life model where distinct species evolve independently, offering a vision of human evolution as more of a braided stream than a solitary branch (Reich, 2018).

Beyond these deep-time revelations, Reich's work offers startling insights into the development of one of humanity's most mysterious and potent tools: language. A key element of this inquiry is the FOXP2 gene, widely recognized for its role in speech and language development. This gene, found not only in modern humans but also in Neanderthals and Denisovans, suggests that our archaic cousins may have had some capacity for vocal communication. However, a pivotal shift occurred around sixty thousand years ago, when modern humans experienced changes that enhanced their ability to produce a wider range of sounds (Gokhman et al., 2020). These changes were not solely genetic; Reich's team also explored epigenetic modifications—alterations in gene expression that influence development without changing the DNA sequence.

Their findings reveal that while Neanderthals and Denisovans shared the FOXP2 gene, their vocal tracts lacked certain adaptations found in modern humans. These adaptations, particularly in the larynx and pharynx, allowed *Homo sapiens* to articulate speech with more complexity. This breakthrough in vocal communication was potentially one of the most significant evolutionary leaps in our species' history, marking the beginning of complex language and the cognitive and cultural evolution that followed (Gokhman et al., 2020).

But why did this happen? What catalyzed this leap in cognitive and cultural evolution? One theory posits that social complexity—driven by larger groups and the need for more sophisticated communication—was the primary driver. As small bands of hunter-gatherers coalesced into larger communities, the ability to share knowledge, plan, and strategize became essential. This cultural innovation, rather than a simple genetic mutation, may have sparked the explosion of modern human behavior that led to art, religion, and eventually civilization.

This leads to a question that has puzzled anthropologists for decades: Why, after hundreds of thousands of years of static existence, did modern humans suddenly outcompete and replace Neanderthals, Denisovans, and other archaic humans? Why did our species—small in number, scattered, and not particularly more intelligent—become the dominant form of life on Earth?

One possibility is sheer chance. Much of human evolution is contingent, a series of fortunate (or unfortunate) events that set the stage for our rise to dominance. A perfect storm of genetic mutations, environmental changes, and cultural innovations—coupled with a series of migrations out of Africa—might have tipped the scales in our favor (Reich, 2018).

Yet, this story is not just one of conquest and replacement. In many ways, the Neanderthals and Denisovans live on in us. Between

2 percent and 5 percent of the DNA in people of non-African descent today comes from Neanderthals, while Denisovan DNA is found in smaller percentages in people from Southeast Asia and Oceania, a geographic and cultural region that includes the islands of the central and southern Pacific Ocean. These genes aren't just curiosities—they may have played a crucial role in our survival, offering genetic advantages that helped early *Homo sapiens* adapt to new environments (Reich, 2018).

Even more puzzling is the fact that archaic human populations, though genetically diverse, were often quite small. Some of the earliest modern human populations in Eurasia might have numbered only in the thousands—hardly enough, it would seem, to dominate an entire continent. And yet they did, spreading out across the globe and absorbing or replacing other human species along the way.

The result of this long and complicated history is the genetic patchwork we see today. South Asians, for example, are a genetic mix of three primary groups: local hunter-gatherers, early farmers from the Harappan civilization, and pastoralists from the Eurasian steppe. This mixture formed the basis of the caste system, which has remained remarkably stable for thousands of years. The caste divisions, still evident in genetic studies, reflect a social structure that froze genetic mixing in place, preserving distinct lineages over millennia.

This complex interplay of genetics, culture, and environment paints a picture of humanity that is far more interconnected—and far more contingent—than ever imagined. Our ancestors were not solitary figures wandering the African savannas; they were part of a vast network of human species, trading genes, ideas, and technologies across continents and millennia. The presence of this ghost species in African DNA also suggests that the migration patterns of early humans were far more complex than previously believed. Rather than a single wave of migration out of Africa, there may have been multiple waves of migration and interaction, with different hominid species contributing to the genetic diversity of modern humans. Could the waves of migration by other hominid species and their eventual colonization and assimilation contributed to the cultural memories and oral traditions that account for what some call the Nephilim? These offspring would have surely been seen as different and perhaps even evil had the mixing been by force or colonization. It has become clear that the story of human evolution, like that of the Anunnaki, is not a simple one. It is a story of adaptation, survival, and sometimes extinction. It's a story where the lines between the ancient and the modern, the human and the nonhuman, blur in ways we are only just beginning to understand.

A World Shattered

The end of the last ice age marked a period of dramatic upheaval as Earth transitioned from a glacial world to the warmer climates we recognize today. This transition, however, was not gradual. Around 12,800 years ago, the sudden and catastrophic event known as the Younger Dryas impact is believed to have triggered a return to near-glacial conditions.

Beneath our feet, the Earth holds secrets. Not just the fossils of long-extinct creatures or the remnants of ancient civilizations, but a deeper, more profound mystery: a rhythm that pulses through the ages, shaping the destiny of our world and all life upon it. This rhythm isn't the steady tick of geological time that most of us learned about in school. It's not the gradual drift of continents or the slow erosion of mountains. Instead, it's a cycle of catastrophe and renewal, of destruction and rebirth, that may have repeated itself many times throughout Earth's long history.

The idea that our planet undergoes periodic cataclysms isn't new. Ancient cultures around the world spoke of great floods, fiery destructions, and times when the sky itself seemed to shift. Modern science has long dismissed these stories as myths or exaggerations of local disasters. But what if there was more to these tales than we've been willing to admit?

Humanity's oldest stories are often tales of destruction and rebirth. From the biblical flood to the Norse Ragnarök, from the Hindu Yugas to the Aztec Five Suns, cultures around the world have preserved memories of world-ending catastrophes and subsequent renewals. For centuries, these stories were dismissed as simple myths, attempts by ancient peoples to explain natural disasters or to convey moral lessons. But a closer examination reveals striking similarities across cultures that had no known contact with each other. These commonalities suggest a shared experience, a global event—or series of events—so profound that it left an indelible mark on the collective human psyche.

Consider the flood myths. While Noah's ark may be the best-known version in Western culture, similar stories appear in traditions around the world. The Mesopotamian *Epic of Gilgamesh*, far older than the biblical account, tells of a great flood and a man who builds a boat to survive it. In ancient Greece, Deucalion and Pyrrha repopulate the world after Zeus floods it to punish human wickedness. The Aztecs believed the world had been destroyed by water and would be again. Even indigenous Australian traditions speak of a time when the seas rose and drowned the land. These flood myths often share specific details: a divine decision to destroy humanity, a warning given to a chosen individual or family, instructions to build a vessel, and the eventual receding of the waters to reveal a changed world. The persistence of these elements across diverse cultures suggests more than coincidence.

Yet floods aren't the only recurring theme in these ancient catastrophe myths. Many traditions speak of times when the sky itself seemed to change. In Chinese mythology, the divine archer Yi shoots down nine of ten suns that have appeared in the sky, saving the world from burning. Plato's account of Atlantis, relayed to him by Egyptian priests, speaks of a time when "the stars revolted," followed by earthquakes and floods that sank the fabled civilization.

Native American traditions are particularly rich in stories of cosmic upheaval. The Hopi speak of previous worlds destroyed by fire and ice before the current one. The Pawnee tell of a time when the north and south stars changed places. And numerous indigenous cultures in both North and South America have legends of long nights or days when the sun didn't rise, followed by a new world dawn. These stories of cosmic disorder often coincide with accounts of the Earth itself being reshaped. Mountains rise, islands sink, and the land is torn asunder. The world that emerges from these cataclysms is invariably different from what came before, often with new species of plants and animals, new landscapes, and new challenges for the survivors.

Archaeological findings from Shanidar Cave in Iraq present a fascinating correlation of data. A team from the Smithsonian Institution, under the leadership of Ralph S. Solecki and in partnership with Iraqi antiquities authorities, conducted excavations at this site. The results of Carbon-14 dating revealed an intriguing pattern in the cave's stratified layers. These layers align closely with the timing of major cataclysmic events, occurring approximately 7,000, 11,500, 18,500, and 29,000 years ago (Thomas, 1963).

Perhaps the most striking discovery was the absence of Carbon-14 deposits during a specific period known as the Caspian Sea North Polar Era, which lasted from about 29,000 to 18,500 years ago. This gap in the geological record can be reasonably attributed to the cave's location during that time. It's likely that Shanidar Cave was situated near the North Pole and consequently sealed beneath a polar ice cap. This environment would have prevented the accumulation of organic matter capable of absorbing Carbon-14, resulting in a period devoid of datable material. In essence, Shanidar Cave stands as a natural archive, silently documenting the last four major cataclysms. Its geological layers tell a story similar to that of other ancient sites, such as Tiwanaku, offering valuable insights into Earth's tumultuous past.

For most of modern history, tales of great floods and global catastrophes were seen as nothing more than imaginative fiction. But as we've begun to uncover evidence of rapid climate shifts, mass extinctions, and sudden geological changes in Earth's past, some researchers have started to look at these ancient stories with fresh eyes. Could these myths be garbled memories of real events? Might they preserve, in symbolic form, a record of catastrophic changes that reshaped our world in the distant past? And if so, what might they tell us about the cycles of destruction and renewal that may govern our planet?

To answer these questions, we need to look beyond mythology and into the realms of geology, astronomy, and physics. We need to examine the evidence written in stone, ice, and the very atoms of our world, and we need to consider some ideas that challenge everything we think we know about Earth's history and its future. When we look at the world around us, it's easy to assume that the Earth changes slowly. Mountains erode grain by grain, continents drift inches per year, and new species evolve over millions of years. This view of gradual change, known as *uniformitarianism*, has been the dominant paradigm in geology for over two centuries. However, the closer we look at the Earth's history, the more we find evidence of sudden, dramatic changes that don't fit neatly into this slow-and-steady model.

In recent decades, a growing body of evidence has begun to suggest that Earth's history may be punctuated by regular, devastating events that reshape the face of our planet. These aren't the slow changes we typically associate with geology, but rapid, violent shifts that could rewrite the map of the world in a matter of days or even hours.

While the most striking example is the Younger Dryas event, as we've mentioned, the geologic record is full of such events:

- **The Paleocene-Eocene Thermal Maximum (PETM):** About 56 million years ago, global temperatures spiked by five to eight degrees Celsius in just a few thousand years, radically reshaping ecosystems around the world.

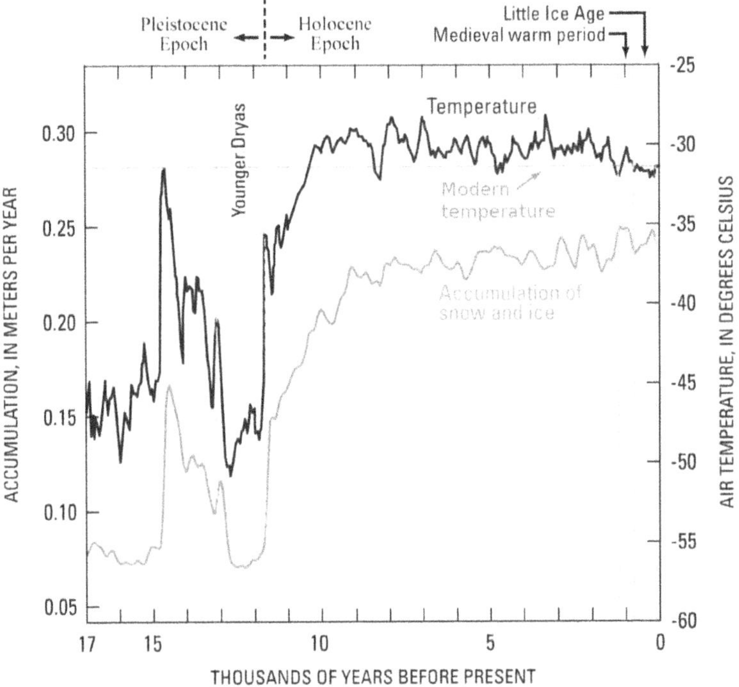

This graph illustrates temperature variations during the Younger Dryas period and the onset of the Holocene, providing key data for understanding climate shifts in Earth's history.

- **The Carnian Pluvial Event (CPE):** This period of extreme climate change about 232 million years ago saw the Earth alternate between arid and ultra-humid conditions, coinciding with a major diversification of dinosaurs and the origin of many modern animal groups.
- **The Great Oxygenation Event (GOE):** Around 2.4 billion years ago, the Earth's atmosphere was transformed by the emergence of oxygen-producing organisms, leading to a mass extinction of anaerobic life and setting the stage for complex multicellular life.

These events, and many others like them, suggest that Earth's history is punctuated by periods of rapid, sometimes catastrophic change. But what could cause such dramatic shifts? One controversial theory, proposed by geologist Robert Schoch and others, suggests that some of these events may have been triggered by solar outbursts—massive eruptions from the sun that bombarded the Earth with charged particles and radiation. Such an event could potentially explain the rapid melting of ice sheets, dramatic climate shifts, and even the scorching of the Earth's surface that some researchers claim to have found evidence for in ancient sites.

Another possibility is that the Earth undergoes periodic crustal displacements—rapid movements of the entire outer shell of the planet over its interior. This idea, first proposed by Charles Hapgood and supported by Albert Einstein, suggests that the accumulation of ice at the poles could occasionally cause the Earth's crust to slip, moving entire continents from polar to tropical latitudes (or vice versa) in a matter of days or weeks.

While mainstream geology has largely rejected Hapgood's theory, it's worth noting that we have evidence of similarly dramatic events in Earth's past. The geological phenomenon known as "true polar wander," for instance, involves the entire solid Earth rotating with respect to its spin axis. Evidence suggests this has happened multiple times in Earth's history, though over much longer timescales than Hapgood proposed.

Perhaps most intriguingly, recent research has begun to reveal evidence of cyclic patterns in Earth's geological history. A 2018 study published in the journal *Geoscience Frontiers* found evidence of a 27.5-million-year cycle of geological activity, marked by clusters of major events including volcanic eruptions, mass extinctions, plate reorganizations, and sea level changes.

The CIA's "Adam and Eve Story"

In 1963, a book was published that would challenge conventional understanding of Earth's history and future. *The Adam and Eve Story*, by Chan Thomas, presented a theory of periodic cataclysms so devastating that they could reset human civilization in a matter of days. While many such fringe theories have come and gone without notice, this one caught the attention of an unlikely reader: the Central Intelligence Agency.

The CIA's interest in the book is a matter of public record. In 2013, the agency declassified a heavily redacted version of *The Adam and Eve Story*, sparking intense speculation about its contents and significance. Why would an intelligence agency be interested in a book about geological catastrophes? What information might it contain that was deemed sensitive enough to classify? Declassified portions of the book, along with other writings by Thomas, outline a theory of periodic pole shifts that aligns in many ways with Hapgood's crustal displacement hypothesis.

According to Thomas, the Earth undergoes a catastrophic pole shift approximately every 11,500 years. During these events, he claimed, the entire crust of the Earth slips over its core in a matter of hours. The results would be devastating: supersonic winds, massive tidal waves, and the shifting of entire continents to new latitudes. Thomas's scenario reads like a Hollywood disaster movie:

> *With a rumble so low as to be inaudible, growing, throbbing, then fuming into a thundering roar, the earthquake starts . . . only it's not like any earthquake in recorded history. In California, the mountains shake like ferns in a breeze; the mighty Pacific rears back and piles up into a mountain of water more than two miles high, then starts its race eastward. With the force of a thousand armies the wind attacks, ripping, shredding everything in its supersonic bombardment. The unbelievable mountain of Pacific seawater follows the wind eastward, burying Los Angeles and San Francisco as if they were but grains of sand (Thomas, 1963).*

While this description may seem far-fetched, it's worth noting that we have evidence of similarly rapid and dramatic changes in Earth's past. The Younger Dryas event, which we discussed earlier, saw temperatures in Greenland drop by up to fifteen degrees Celsius in a matter of decades. And we know that Earth's magnetic field has reversed many times throughout its history, sometimes quite rapidly. Thomas claimed that these pole shifts were triggered by an interaction between the Earth's core and cosmic forces, possibly related to the planet's movement through the galaxy.

Mainstream geology rejects the idea of such rapid crustal displacements, but some researchers have proposed mechanisms by which significant shifts could occur more quickly than conventionally thought. For instance, a 2018 study in the journal *Earth and Planetary Science Letters* suggested that shifts in Earth's axis of rotation could occur over centuries or even decades in response to the melting of ice sheets. Perhaps the most intriguing aspect of *The Adam and Eve Story* is not its geological theories, but its hints at hidden knowledge (Thomas, 1963).

Consider the Great Sphinx of Giza. Conventional Egyptology dates it to around 2500 BCE, but some researchers argue that its weathering patterns indicate a much older origin. Schoch, a geologist by training, contends that the Sphinx bears marks of water erosion that could only have occurred during a much wetter climate period, potentially pushing its construction back to the end of the last ice age.

This revised timeline, if accurate, would revolutionize our understanding of ancient history. It would suggest that an advanced civilization existed thousands of years earlier than we thought possible, one with the knowledge and capability to create monumental architecture that has endured for millennia. The implications go beyond just pushing back the timeline of human achievement. If these ancient builders did indeed possess advanced knowledge, what else might they have known? And more importantly, what might they have been trying to tell us?

Many ancient monuments exhibit an obsession with celestial alignments and cycles. The Great Pyramid of Giza, for instance, is aligned with remarkable precision to the cardinal directions. Stonehenge in England tracks solar and lunar cycles with incredible accuracy. And sites like Göbekli Tepe in Turkey, dated to around 10,000 BCE, show a level of astronomical knowledge that seems far beyond what hunter-gatherer societies should possess.

These alignments and astronomical markers could be more than just calendars or religious symbols. They could be warnings, a way for ancient people to track long-term celestial cycles that might herald times of great change or danger. The Maya Long Count calendar, famously misinterpreted as predicting the end of the world in 2012, actually tracks several interlocking cosmic cycles. The longest of these, the baktun, lasts 144,000 days or about 394 years. Thirteen baktuns make up a Great Cycle of roughly 5,125 years.

Interestingly, the end of the last Great Cycle in 2012 coincided with the alignment of the December solstice sun with the galactic equator, an event that occurs only once every 25,772 years due to the precession of the equinoxes. While this alignment didn't bring about the end of the world, it does raise questions about what the Maya might have believed about these grand cosmic cycles. Other ancient cultures show a similar preoccupation with vast spans of time. Hindu cosmology speaks of Yugas, cosmic ages that repeat in cycles of millions of years. The ancient Egyptians referred to a time known as Zep Tepi, the "First Time," a golden age from which all their knowledge descended.

These traditions of lost golden ages and recurring cycles of destruction and renewal echo through cultures around the world. But are they merely myths, or could they be distorted memories of real events? The idea of a technologically advanced ancient civilization that was nearly wiped out by a global catastrophe might seem like the stuff of science fiction. But it's worth remembering that our own civilization, for all its technological marvels, is remarkably fragile. A sufficiently large solar flare, asteroid impact, or other cosmic event could potentially plunge us back into a preindustrial state within days. If such an event happened in the distant past, how long would it take for the survivors to rebuild? And how much of their advanced knowledge might be lost or distorted in the process? "Yes, Noah, Adam and Eve, Osiris, Ta'aroa, Zeus, and Vishnu have much deeper meaning now; and, as they join hands and walk with us, we hear Adam and Eve saying: 'Listen—for now we can truly share our story with you" (Thomas, 1963).

If Thomas's book contained nothing but groundless speculation, why would it interest the CIA, let alone be classified? Foreknowledge of a coming catastrophe, even if it were centuries away, could significantly influence long-term policy decisions. It could drive investment in certain technologies, shape decisions about resource allocation, and even influence geopolitical strategies. Moreover, if there was evidence of advanced ancient civilizations or technologies, it could have profound implications for national security. Imagine the strategic advantage that could be gained from rediscovering lost technologies or deciphering ancient warnings about cosmic threats.

Our planet doesn't exist in isolation. It's part of a vast, dynamic universe, subject to forces and influences that we're only beginning to understand. And some of these cosmic factors may play a crucial role in shaping the cycles of catastrophe and renewal that we've been exploring. Furthermore, some researchers suggest that these cosmic cycles might also operate on shorter timescales, in ways that could affect us more directly. Which brings us to one of the most controversial and intriguing ideas in the study of Earth cycles: the possibility of rapid, civilization-altering catastrophes.

Such a catastrophe, possibly caused by a comet or an asteroid striking the Earth, led to massive floods, wildfires, and the rapid extinction of ice age megafauna across the globe (Firestone et al., 2007). But it wasn't just animals that perished. Entire human populations were displaced, their homes destroyed, and their cultures erased from the face of the Earth. This event, more than any other, imprinted a deep trauma on the collective consciousness of our ancestors.

Imagine the survivors of this cataclysm: Once secure in their world, they suddenly found themselves adrift, navigating a landscape of loss and devastation. These were not just people with memories; they were a species scarred by trauma. The Younger Dryas impact was a formative moment, shaping the human psyche and, in turn, influencing the development of early civilizations. As these displaced groups migrated in search of stability, they carried with them not just their physical possessions but also the weight of their collective experience. This trauma forged a culture that was deeply introspective, spiritually inclined, and driven by a need to remember and preserve their knowledge.

Climate Refugees

In the wake of the Younger Dryas impact event, our world was reshaped not only in the physical landscape but also in the cultural and psychological terrain of our ancestors. The extinction of ice age megafauna (perhaps even megahominids) forced a mass displacement of early human populations, setting the stage for a profound transformation in human consciousness and culture. Our ancestors emerged from this crucible not merely as a "species with amnesia," as Graham Hancock (1995) suggests, but as a species bearing the deep scars of collective trauma. This trauma became the driving force behind a cultural revolution that would define the course of human civilization for millennia to come.

Archaeological and genetic evidence demonstrates that contact between the Near East, the Caucasus, the Steppe, and Central Europe occurred as early as the fifth millennium BCE. This interaction intensified during the fourth millennium BCE with the advent of new technologies, including the wheel, wagon, copper alloys, new weapons, and domesticated breeds of sheep. These developments were pivotal in shaping the cultural and genetic landscape of the Yamnaya complex on the Eurasian Steppe, with about half of the Yamnaya's Bronze Age ancestry believed to have originated from the Caucasus. In the third millennium BCE, the increased mobility brought about by wheeled transport and the rise of pastoralism led to significant population expansions linked to the Yamnaya, including the domestication of horses, which facilitated more effective management of larger herds. These migrations and expansions significantly influenced the genetic makeup of contemporary European and South Asian populations, underscoring the Caucasus region's crucial role in the prehistoric formation of Eurasian genetic diversity.

As we consider the origins and movements of the Yamnaya people, it's worth exploring the possibility that their ancestors might have migrated from regions further north or northeast around twelve thousand years ago, during the dramatic climatic shifts at the end of the last ice age. The retreat of the glaciers and the onset of the Holocene likely triggered significant migrations as human populations adapted to the changing environment. Some groups, who had previously been confined to the harsher northern climates, could have moved southward into the Pontic-Caspian steppe as the world warmed. These migrations may have introduced new technologies, cultural practices, and genetic lineages into the region, setting the stage for the emergence of the Yamnaya culture.

David Reich's research has provided strong genetic evidence supporting the idea that the Yamnaya people were instrumental in spreading Indo-European languages across Europe, a finding that challenges the Anatolian hypothesis. The Anatolian hypothesis posits that Indo-European languages spread primarily through early agriculturalists from Anatolia around eight thousand to nine thousand years ago. Reich's findings, however, suggest that a significant migration from the Pontic-Caspian steppe during the Bronze Age, led by the Yamnaya, played a more crucial role in this linguistic spread. This genetic evidence bolsters the Kurgan hypothesis and aligns with the idea that the Yamnaya and their predecessors could have been influenced by earlier northern populations, further complicating the narrative of human migration and cultural diffusion in prehistoric Eurasia.

A Shared Ancestor

The Kurgan hypothesis and the Anatolian hypothesis are two competing theories that attempt to explain the origin and spread of the Proto-Indo-European (PIE) language, which is the hypothetical common ancestor of the Indo-European language family. The Kurgan hypothesis, proposed by Marija Gimbutas in the 1950s, suggests that the PIE language originated in the Pontic-Caspian steppe region (present-day Ukraine and southern Russia) during the Chalcolithic period (between 4000 and 3500 BCE). According to this theory, the PIE language was spoken by the Kurgan culture, named after their distinctive burial mounds (kurgans). The Kurgan people were nomadic pastoralists who domesticated the horse and invented the wheel. Gimbutas argued that the Kurgan culture expanded westward and eastward during the fourth and third millennia BCE, spreading their language and culture through conquest and migration. This expansion is believed to have led to the differentiation of PIE into various branches, such as Celtic, Germanic, Slavic, and Indo-Iranian.

On the other hand, the Anatolian hypothesis, proposed by Colin Renfrew in the 1980s, argues that the PIE language originated in Anatolia (present-day Turkey) between 7000 and 6000 BCE, during the early Neolithic period. This theory is based on the idea that the spread of agriculture from Anatolia to Europe and Asia coincided with the dispersal of the PIE language. According to Renfrew, the Neolithic farmers from Anatolia gradually migrated to other regions, taking their language with them. The discovery of Neolithic sites like Göbekli Tepe and Karahan Tepe in southeastern Turkey, which date back to around 9000 BCE, has been used to support the idea of an advanced Anatolian civilization that could have been the source of the PIE language.

The primary distinction between the Anatolian and Kurgan hypotheses lies in their proposed timeframes and mechanisms for PIE dispersal. The Anatolian hypothesis suggests PIE spread gradually with agricultural diffusion from Anatolia beginning around 7000 BCE. The Kurgan hypothesis instead proposes a later, more rapid expansion from the Pontic-Caspian steppe between 4000 and 3000 BCE, driven by mobile pastoralism, horse domestication, and wheeled transport.

While each theory addresses the same archaeological puzzle, mounting evidence increasingly supports the Kurgan model. Recent ancient DNA studies reveal a substantial influx of steppe ancestry into Central and Western Europe during the Bronze Age, precisely when the Kurgan expansion would have occurred. This genetic evidence, combined with archaeological data on horse domestication and the spread of chariot technology, aligns more convincingly with the Kurgan timeline than with the earlier Neolithic agricultural dispersal. The Kurgan hypothesis therefore provides the most coherent explanation for PIE origins, though some scholars continue exploring integrative approaches that might reconcile elements of both models. Additionally, the Kurgan hypothesis aligns better with the reconstructed vocabulary of PIE. The PIE language has many words related to horse domestication, wheeled vehicles, and pastoral nomadism, which are more consistent with the Kurgan culture of the Pontic-Caspian steppe than with the agricultural societies of Anatolia. For example, the PIE word for "wheel" (**kwékwlos*) is believed to have originated from the Kurgan culture, as they were among the earliest to use wheeled vehicles.

Second, archaeological evidence supports the idea of a significant expansion of the Kurgan culture during the fourth and third millennia BCE. The spread of kurgan burials, as well as the dispersal of a new type of pottery and other cultural markers, coincides with the proposed timeframe for the diversification of PIE into its various branches. In contrast, the Anatolian hypothesis relies more on the idea of a gradual diffusion of language through the spread of agriculture, which is less well-supported by archaeological findings.

Third, recent genetic studies have provided substantial evidence in favor of the Kurgan hypothesis. Analysis of ancient DNA from human remains has shown a significant influx of genes from the Pontic-Caspian steppe into Europe during the Bronze Age, coinciding with the spread of Indo-European languages. This genetic evidence suggests that the Kurgan people played a crucial role in shaping the genetic and linguistic landscape of Europe and Asia.

While the Anatolian hypothesis offers an alternative perspective on the origins of PIE, the Kurgan hypothesis remains the more widely accepted theory among scholars. The combination of linguistic, archaeological, and genetic evidence lends strong support to the idea that the PIE language originated in the Pontic-Caspian steppe and spread through the expansions of the Kurgan culture. As research continues, the Kurgan hypothesis may be further refined, but it currently provides the most comprehensive and well-supported explanation for the origin and dispersal of the Indo-European language family, and possibly the missing link to the Sumerian Problem.

Ancient North Eurasians (ANE)

One of the key findings from Reich's work is the identification of a previously unknown population called the Ancient North Eurasians (ANE). This group, represented by specimens such as the Mal'ta boy found in Siberia and dated to around twenty-four thousand years ago, contributed significantly to the genetic makeup of both Native Americans *and* Europeans. The ANE ancestry is crucial in understanding the northern genetic component that later appeared in steppe populations.

Reich's team identified another important population group called the eastern hunter-gatherers (EHG). These people, found in western Russia and dated to around 6000–5000 BCE, carried a substantial proportion of ANE ancestry. The EHG thus served as a vector, bringing genetic material from northern populations, including Siberia, into the steppe region. This occurred well before the formation of the Yamnaya culture, which is typically associated with the early Bronze Age and often linked to early Indo-European speakers.

The Yamnaya people, who lived on the Pontic-Caspian steppe around 3300–2600 BCE, were found to have derived their ancestry from at least two distinct sources. One of these was the EHG, carrying the northern genetic component. The other was a population related to people of the Caucasus and Iran. This mixing event, which formed the Yamnaya, represents a crucial moment in the genetic history of the steppe, blending northern and southern ancestries and playing a significant role in the spread of Indo-European languages.

These findings support the idea that people from further north, including regions of Russia and Siberia, indeed contributed genetically to the populations of the steppe before the Bronze Age. The northern genetic component, originally derived from ANE populations, was already present in the EHG.

Tarim Mummies

The ANE ancestry is crucial in understanding the northern genetic component that later appeared in steppe populations.

This discovery by Reich and his colleagues provides a new context for interpreting the origins and characteristics of the Tarim mummies. The *Tarim mummies* are remarkably well-preserved human remains found in the arid Tarim Basin of what is now western China, dating from around 2100 BCE to 200 CE. Clad in finely woven woolen textiles, they possess striking features often described as Western or European-like, such as light-colored hair, elongated skulls, and deep-set eyes. These individuals have long puzzled researchers. Their presence in such an isolated, interior region of Central Asia raises significant questions about prehistoric migrations, ancient trade routes, and the possible movements of early Indo-European-speaking peoples far earlier than once assumed.

Recent genetic studies, particularly those published in 2021, have revealed that the Tarim mummies have a strong genetic affinity with the Ancient North Eurasians. In fact, the Tarim Basin individuals from around 2100–1700 BCE derive approximately 72 percent of their ancestry from ANE-related populations, specifically those represented by the Afontova Gora 3 (AG3) specimen from southern Siberia. The remaining 28 percent of their genetic makeup comes from ANE populations. This genetic profile offers a new explanation for the Western physical features observed in many Tarim mummies, such as their red or blonde hair, deep-set eyes, and high-bridged noses. Rather than being direct evidence of a recent migration from Europe or the Middle East, as was once hypothesized, these traits likely reflect the ANE ancestry preserved in this population (Zhang et al. 2021).

For instance, the famous Beauty of Loulan, dated to around 1800 BCE, is noted for her auburn hair and distinctly non-Asian facial features (Barber, 1999). Similarly, the Cherchen Man (c. 1000 BCE) is described as having red hair and a long nose. The Princess of Xiaohe (c. 1800 BCE) was also found with red hair and long eyelashes (Mair, 2016). Interestingly, the Tarim mummies represent one of the few known Holocene populations that derive the majority of their ancestry from Pleistocene ANE groups. This makes them, in the words of the researchers, "the best representatives" of the Ancient North Eurasians, despite living thousands of years after the original ANE populations (Zhang et al., 2021).

This genetic evidence suggests that the early inhabitants of the Tarim Basin were not recent migrants from the West, as previously thought, but rather descendants of a local population with deep roots in the region. These people appear to have adopted agricultural and pastoral practices from neighboring cultures while remaining genetically isolated, allowing them to preserve their unique genetic heritage. The Tarim mummies thus provide a fascinating window into the complex population history of Central Asia, demonstrating how ancient genetic lineages can persist and express themselves phenotypically long after the original populations have disappeared. Their Western-like features, rather than indicating a recent European migration, actually reflect a much older genetic legacy dating back to the Paleolithic period.

The Sumerian Language Origin

Ancient DNA have clarified several unresolved issues regarding prehistoric cultural and population changes. A notable finding is the cline of European hunter-gatherer ancestry, extending from West to East, which contrasts with the ancestry of early European farmers who were more closely related to Northwest Anatolian farmers and pre-agricultural populations from the Levant. Historically, the Near East and Anatolia have been recognized as key regions from which European farming and animal husbandry originated. During the Mesolithic and Early Neolithic periods, two major ancestral populations shaped the genetic landscape of the region. In the west, groups with Anatolian and Levantine ancestry dominated, while in the east, a genetically distinct population emerged. This eastern ancestry was first identified in Upper Pleistocene individuals from the Caucasus region of Georgia, now known as Caucasus hunter-gatherers (CHG), and later in Mesolithic and Neolithic individuals from the Iranian plateau. Over the following millennia, particularly between the Neolithic and Bronze Age, these populations began to intermingle, leading to a more homogenized genetic profile across the region.

Further north, in the Eneolithic and Bronze Age Samara region, individuals dating from approximately 5200 to 4000 BCE carried a balanced mix of Eastern Hunter-Gatherer (EHG) and CHG/Iranian ancestry. This combination is now referred to as "steppe ancestry." The genetic signature associated with the steppe expanded west into Europe, east toward the Altai Mountains, and south into South Asia. These movements had a profound and lasting impact on the genetic structure of many present-day populations (Wang et al., 2019).

Many of these displaced peoples settled in various regions, from the highlands of the Caucasus to the fertile crescent of Mesopotamia. One such group was the Kura-Araxes culture, which emerged around 3500 BCE in the mountainous regions of the South Caucasus. The Kura-Araxes were a resilient people, adept at metalwork, agriculture, and pottery (Kohl, 2009). As they spread southward, they encountered other cultures, including those in southern Mesopotamia. For a long time, researchers thought these two groups—the Kura-Araxes and the Sumerians—were completely separate. New evidence suggests they might have more in common than we thought.

The Urartian language provides a fascinating link between the ancient cultures of the Caucasus and Mesopotamia. Like Sumerian, Urartian was written using a variant of the cuneiform script, specifically the Neo-Assyrian cuneiform. This shared writing system is a tangible connection between these cultures, suggesting a common heritage or at least significant cultural exchange. Attested from the late ninth century to the late seventh century BCE, Urartian served as the official written language of the state of Urartu. The language is closely related to Hurrian, with both belonging to the Hurro-Urartian language family. This family may have its roots in the Kura-Araxes culture, which flourished in the Caucasus region around 3500 BCE.

A shocking study by Alexei Kassian (2014) found surprising similarities between the Sumerian language and a group of languages called Hurro-Urartian, which were spoken in the same areas where the Kura-Araxes culture had spread. Some basic words, like those for "dog," "hand," and "meat," sound very similar in both languages, hinting at a possible shared linguistic heritage.

Kassian suggests that this similarity might be because of ancient contact between these groups. Perhaps as the Kura-Araxes people moved south, they interacted with the early Sumerians, influencing their language and culture. However, the story might go back even further. The same study suggests that Sumerian and Hurro-Urartian languages might have split from a common source as far back as 12,000 BCE (Kassian, 2014), within a striking margin of error of Younger Dryas impact, long before writing was invented, during a time when the last ice age was ending and people were just beginning to develop agriculture, which could mean that the ancestors of both the Sumerians and the Kura-Araxes people once shared a common language and culture, far back in *pre*history. As they separated and developed in different regions over thousands of years, they retained some common words and perhaps other cultural elements. This new hypothesis could reshape our understanding of early human migrations and the origins of civilization in the Near East.

The hypothesis of an extinct language of what could be described as a nomadic priest-noble class (perhaps the Anunnaki), becomes more plausible when we consider the linguistic evidence. The Urartian language, like Sumerian, shows some intriguing features that set it apart from other language families in the region. Both Urartian and Sumerian are ergative languages, a relatively rare linguistic feature. They also share agglutinative morphology, where words are formed by stringing together distinct meaningful elements. These structural similarities, combined with the lexical matches found in recent studies, like the one cited previously, suggest a deeper connection between these languages than was previously thought to exist. Furthermore, the Urartian script, like Sumerian cuneiform, was primarily used for royal inscriptions and religious texts. This limited use suggests that the writing system may have been the domain of a specialized class of scribes or priests, supporting the idea of a priestly class maintaining and transmitting ancient linguistic traditions.

The Cuneiform Connection

The adaptation of cuneiform for Urartian follows a pattern seen across the ancient Near East. Just as Akkadian, Hittite, and other languages adopted and adapted cuneiform, so did Urartian. This process of adaptation often involved simplification and standardization of the script to suit the needs of the new language. In Urartian, each cuneiform sign typically expresses a single sound value, a simplification from the more complex Sumerian and Akkadian systems. This standardization might reflect the work of scribes or priests who were tasked with adapting the writing system to their language, possibly drawing on older traditions preserved by a wandering priestly class.

This shared use of cuneiform across different languages and cultures in the ancient Near East points to a complex network of cultural and linguistic exchange. It suggests the existence of a class of educated scribes or priests who were capable of adapting this writing system to new languages, potentially preserving older linguistic traditions in the process.

The hypothesis of an extinct priestly language offers a compelling explanation for these connections. Such a language could have served as a bridge between the earlier, pre-catastrophe linguistic landscape and the later attested languages like Sumerian and Urartian. This could explain both the sudden appearance of complex linguistic systems in the historical record and the puzzling connections between geographically distant language groups.

For years, scholars have viewed the Sumerians as a mysterious and isolated group, whose sudden appearance in the historical record has been difficult to explain. This Sumerian Problem has puzzled researchers, who have struggled to understand how such an advanced civilization could have emerged seemingly out of nowhere. But recent linguistic studies suggest that the Sumerians were not as isolated as once thought.

If we consider the possibility that the Sumerians and the Kura-Araxes people both descended from a common cultural and linguistic source, the Sumerian Problem becomes less of a mystery. Instead, we see a more interconnected world, where migration, trade, and cultural exchange played a crucial role in the development of early civilizations. The Kura-Araxes people, driven by the trauma of their past, may have carried with them not only their skills and knowledge but also a deep-seated need to preserve their culture through oral traditions, rituals, and spiritual practices.

Clues to the ritual and spiritual practices of these early people may be found in their agricultural practices. Recent studies, such as those outlined in *The Antiquity and Domestication of the Opium Poppy* (Salavert et al., 2020), suggest that the domestication of the opium poppy (*Papaver somniferum*) began in the western Mediterranean around 5600 BCE, with its rapid spread into temperate Europe soon after. The earliest confirmed cultivation belongs to Neolithic farming populations, descendants of the Upper Paleolithic Europeans often referred to as Cro-Magnon. It is possible that the knowledge of the plant predates its formal domestication. Upper Paleolithic hunter-gatherers may have encountered and experimented with wild poppies long before they were cultivated, passing down a legacy of botanical awareness that their Neolithic descendants eventually formalized into agricultural practice.

The Antiquity and Domestication of the Opium Poppy

As we've seen represented in the art of Mesopotamia and beyond, the opium poppy has a long history of human use and cultivation, stretching back thousands of years. As one of the earliest domesticated plants outside the Fertile Crescent, the opium poppy presents an intriguing case study in early agriculture and the spread of domesticated species across Europe. Recent archaeological and morphometric studies have provided new insights into the origins and domestication of this historically significant and controversial plant. By directly dating ancient poppy seeds and applying advanced shape analysis techniques, researchers have gained fresh insights into when and where opium poppies were first cultivated and how they spread across Europe during the Neolithic period.

The wild progenitor of the opium poppy, *Papaver setigerum*, is native to the western Mediterranean region, including parts of Spain, France, Italy, and North Africa (Zohary et al., 2012). This distribution suggests that the opium poppy was likely first domesticated in this area, rather than in Southwest Asia like many other early crops (Salavert et al., 2020). However, pinpointing exactly where and when domestication occurred has proven challenging. Some of the earliest proposed evidence for opium poppy use comes from Neolithic sites in the Near East and Anatolia, with poppy seeds reportedly found at the Pre-Pottery Neolithic sites of Atlit-Yam in Israel and Körtik Tepe in Turkey (Kislev et al., 2004; Rössner et al., 2018). These early finds are now viewed skeptically by many researchers, who suggest that these seeds may be intrusive from later cultural layers, especially given the lack of wild opium poppies in this region today and the absence of additional evidence from extensive archaeobotanical work (Salavert et al., 2020).

Instead, the earliest secure evidence for opium poppy use and possible cultivation comes from Neolithic sites in the western Mediterranean dating to the sixth millennium BCE. Notable finds include a single charred poppy seed from the Impressa culture site of Peiro Signado in southern France, dated to around 5885–5720 BCE, and charred poppy capsules from multiple layers at the Cardial culture lake village of La Marmotta in central Italy, with part of the site dated by dendrochronology to 5538–5290 CE (Salavert et al., 2020). These Mediterranean finds fall within the native range of wild poppies, making it difficult to determine if they represent gathered wild plants or early cultivation. However, the presence of capsule fragments at La Marmotta and the ubiquity of poppy remains at some sites suggest that deliberate cultivation was likely occurring by this time (Rottoli and Pessina, 2007; Antolín, 2016).

From its early center of use in the Mediterranean, opium poppy cultivation spread rapidly into temperate regions of central and northern Europe. Poppy seeds begin appearing at sites associated with the Linearbandkeramik (LBK) culture in central Europe around 5300–5200 BCE (Salavert et al., 2020). This early adoption of poppy cultivation by LBK farmers, outside the natural range of wild poppies, represents one of the earliest examples of poppy use in a fully agricultural context.

Early LBK finds come from sites in Germany like Vaihingen an der Enz and Nieder-Mörlen, with poppy seeds found in features dated to the Flomborn phase (LBK II) around 5350–5200 BCE (Bogaard et al., 2013; Kreuz et al., 2005). Poppy seeds are also documented from early LBK sites in the Netherlands, such as Geleen-Janskamperveld, dated to around 5200–5000 BCE (Bakels, 2007). The appearance of opium poppy at these sites from the beginning of regional LBK occupation suggests it was part of the initial crop package brought by early farmers as they colonized new areas.

The sudden appearance of opium poppy in the LBK culture, far from its Mediterranean origins, prompts questions about how it spread. Evidence of direct contact between Cardial and LBK populations around 5300–5200 BCE suggests that interactions between these communities likely facilitated the northward spread of poppy cultivation (Salavert et al., 2020). The plant's adaptability may have also played a role, allowing it to thrive in a broad range of soil types and climates, making it an attractive crop for early farmers in new territories.

Interestingly, while opium poppy was adopted early by LBK farmers, other typically Mediterranean crops like naked wheat varieties are only found occasionally in late LBK contexts (Salavert et al., 2020). This suggests that opium poppy may have been viewed as particularly desirable compared to other Mediterranean domesticates, possibly filling an important economic or cultural niche for early temperate European farmers.

Recent studies have revolutionized our understanding of opium poppy domestication in Neolithic Europe. Aurélie Salavert and colleagues (2020) used advanced radiocarbon dating techniques to establish a chronology for early poppy use, confirming cultivation in the western Mediterranean by at least 5600 BCE, with rapid spread into temperate Europe around 5300–5200 BCE.

Ana Jesus and fellow researchers (2021) developed morphometric analyses to distinguish between wild and domesticated poppy seeds. Their findings suggest domestication was a gradual process, with mixed populations persisting for over a millennium after initial cultivation. The opium poppy's versatility likely contributed to its popularity among early farmers. As David Merlin (1984) notes, it provided food, medicine, and possibly played a role in rituals. Its hardiness and adaptability facilitated its spread across diverse environments. The poppy's journey from western Europe to the Fertile Crescent may have been facilitated by early human migrations. As it reached Mesopotamia, emerging civilizations like the Sumerians likely adopted and integrated it into their agricultural and cultural practices.

This connection between early European farmers and the Sumerians, linked by the opium poppy, suggests a broader network of knowledge exchange in prehistory. It challenges the notion of Sumerian advancements as solely indigenous developments, instead placing them within a larger context of cultural and technological diffusion that began millennia earlier, possibly even before the climatic changes following the Younger Dryas event.

A New Understanding of Ancient Civilization

The theory that the Sumerians were influenced by the Kura-Araxes culture, and that both groups shared a common linguistic and cultural heritage that dates back to 12,000 BCE, provides a new lens through which to view the origins of civilization in the Near East. It suggests that the Sumerian Problem may not be a problem at all but rather a reflection of our limited understanding of the deep and complex connections between ancient cultures. These connections were not merely the result of material exchange but were rooted in shared experiences of trauma and survival. The catastrophic events of the Younger Dryas period, the displacement of peoples, and the loss of material culture forced these ancient peoples to find new ways to preserve their knowledge and identity. They did so through oral tradition, through music, through ritual, and through the careful transmission of sacred plants like the poppy through ritual and practice.

In this light, the Sumerians and their contemporaries were not isolated cultures that sprang up independently in different parts of the world. They were part of a broader, interconnected web of human experience, one that stretches back to the end of the last ice age. This web was woven from the threads of shared trauma, collective memory, and the deep human need to connect with the divine and with each other after severe climatic instability forced many human groups to migrate in search of more hospitable environments. Among these migrating peoples were groups from the highlands of the South Caucasus and adjacent regions, which include parts of modern-day Armenia, Georgia, and Azerbaijan. These regions, rich in resources and with a burgeoning Neolithic culture, were home to early agriculturalists and proto-metallurgists. As the climate worsened, these highland communities faced increasing pressure to find more sustainable living conditions. Compelled by necessity, some groups ventured southward, crossing the formidable barriers of the Zagros Mountains. These migrating people may have been the Shulaveri-Shomu culture (6000 BC–5000 BCE), known for their early advances in agriculture, winemaking, domestication of animals, irrigation, and rudimentary metallurgy. Their journey over the mountains was arduous but driven by the knowledge that survival lay in more temperate and fertile lands.

Arriving in the Mesopotamian plain, these highland migrants encountered the semi-settled peoples of the Ubaid culture. The Ubaid people, already practicing a basic form of agriculture and animal husbandry, were significantly impacted by the newcomers. The migrants from the highlands brought with them advanced agricultural techniques, including irrigation and crop cultivation, which were far more developed than those of the indigenous Mesopotamians. They also introduced early metallurgical skills, allowing for the creation of more efficient tools and weapons, which seemed almost magical to the local population.

Where Heaven and Earth Met: Mount Hermon

The story of the Anunnaki and the establishment of Kharsag—the Sumerian equivalent to the Biblical Garden in Eden—has long been overshadowed by religious interpretations, obscuring the historical and agricultural aspects of this ancient settlement. Early translations of Sumerian tablets, such as those by George A. Barton (1918) in his book *Miscellaneous Babylonian Inscriptions* and later Samuel Noah Kramer's (1963) misinterpreted much of the content due to religious biases and linguistic challenges. However, with more careful analysis and attention to Sumerian ideograms and grammar, Christian O'Brien's secular analysis (1997) of this material can help reconstruct a clearer narrative that reveals the Anunnaki as agricultural and societal benefactors—nomadic, displaced shamans who brought vital knowledge to early human societies.

Kharsag

At the heart of this narrative is Kharsag, a settlement located in a mountainous region near modern-day Lebanon and Syria. The term *Kharsag*, which translates to "principal, fenced enclosure," referred to a highly cultivated and irrigated settlement, meticulously planned by the Anunnaki to support agricultural operations. This area was later referred to as the Garden in Eden by the Hebrews. The Sumerian syllable *gar*, which has survived in modern English as "garden," underscores the agricultural focus of this settlement.

According to the Kharsag Epics, the Anunnaki descended from the "Heavens" to establish this settlement, where they introduced agricultural techniques to the local, primitive tribes. The epics describe their arrival as a moment where "Heaven and Earth met," a poetic reference to their descent from the skies into the mountainous terrain. The Anunnaki, led by Enlil and supported by other key figures like Enki and Ninhursag, organized and managed the agricultural efforts that transformed the land. Mount Hermon held particular geographic significance as their chosen site. This towering peak symbolized a connection between the earthly and celestial realms, an association that aligns with the Hebraic account in the Book of Enoch, where angels descend onto the mountain's summit. Beyond its symbolic importance, Mount Hermon offered practical advantages: Its fertile foothills and proximity to water sources provided ideal conditions for the agricultural innovations the Anunnaki were about to introduce.

Misinterpretations of the Tablets

Early translations of the Sumerian tablets led to widespread misunderstandings of key terms. For instance, the Sumerian term *dingir* was often translated as "god," which obscured the original meaning of "lord" or "shining one," a term applied to the Anunnaki. This translation error contributed to the mythologization of the Anunnaki as deities. However, when viewed through a more accurate linguistic lens, they emerge not as divine figures but as displaced leaders—nomadic, post–ice age shamans bringing their knowledge of plants, animals, and societal structures to early humans.

One notable misinterpretation was the translation of the Sumerian term *en-ge-li* as "Air God," when it is now believed to translate as "Lord of Cultivation." This led to confusion about the true role of the Anunnaki in ancient society. The Anunnaki, alongside the Apkallu, acted as mediators between humans and the cosmic forces they represented. The significance of the Apkallu's role becomes even more crucial when considering the Kharsag Epics. These epics suggest that the Anunnaki, displaced by the Younger Dryas climatic changes, sought to bring their advanced knowledge of agriculture, biology, and governance to primitive human societies. The Apkallu served as the conduit for this knowledge transfer, teaching early humans the principles of farming, animal husbandry, and societal organization.

The Anunnaki introduced sophisticated agricultural practices to the region, including the construction of a reservoir and irrigation systems. These innovations allowed for year-round cultivation, even in a region that would have otherwise been dependent on seasonal rainfall. The epics describe how the Anunnaki plowed the land, planted various grains, and established orchards. Livestock, including sheep and cattle, were domesticated and housed in permanent enclosures with running water.

Ninkhursag, who is often referred to as the "Lady of the Mountain," played a crucial role in these developments, using her knowledge of biology and agriculture to increase the yield of crops and ensure the health of the livestock. Enki, known as the "Lord of the Land," managed the operations, while Utu (or Ugmash), later deified by the Babylonians as Shamash, used his knowledge of the sun to aid in surveying and planning the fields.

The Anunnaki's agricultural expertise was not limited to practical applications but extended to a deep understanding of the land. For instance, they constructed windbreaks to protect the crops and planted trees strategically to provide shade. They also built permanent structures to house themselves and their livestock, reflecting a commitment to the long-term success of the settlement.

The Council of Seven and Governance

The Anunnaki were organized democratically, with a Council of Seven making major decisions. This council, which included Enlil, Ninkhursag, Enki, and others, periodically met in a council chamber within the Mountain House at Kharsag. The Supreme Commander, Anu, sometimes joined these meetings, paralleling the Hebrew tradition of the "Most High" and the Council of Seven Archangels.

The Kharsag Epics provide insight into the governance of the settlement, showing how decisions were made to ensure the prosperity of the people. For example, it was in one such council meeting that Ninkhursag argued passionately for the construction of a reservoir, a decision that proved essential for the success of the settlement. This settlement faced numerous challenges in its early days, including sickness and natural disasters. One epic describes how sickness spread through the settlement, affecting even Enlil and Ninkhursag. Despite these hardships, the Anunnaki overcame the challenges through their advanced knowledge of medicine and agriculture. Ninkhursag, in particular, is credited with developing solutions to the agricultural problems that arose, such as pests and flooding.

Over time, the settlement prospered, with surplus food being produced and shared with the local tribespeople. These tribes, who had previously lived in primitive conditions, learned from the Anunnaki and became integrated into the settlement. The Anunnaki's influence on the local population is evident in their transformation from foragers and hunters into skilled farmers and herders. The Kharsag Epics conclude by emphasizing the lasting impact of the Anunnaki on the region. They did not only cultivate the land but also shaped the future of human civilization. Their contributions to agriculture, governance, and society were so significant that their memory persisted for millennia, eventually becoming intertwined with religious narratives about angels and gods.

The Anunnaki's influence extended beyond the immediate region of Kharsag, as their agricultural and societal practices spread to other parts of the ancient world. Their descendants, both literal and cultural, carried their knowledge to other civilizations, including those in Mesopotamia, where their memory was preserved in Sumerian, Akkadian, and Babylonian texts. The Apkallu, as mediators between the Anunnaki and humanity, played a crucial role in this knowledge transfer. They ensured that the wisdom of the Anunnaki was not lost but passed down through generations, forming the basis of early human civilization. The teachings of the Apkallu encompassed not only practical skills like agriculture and construction but also spiritual and philosophical concepts that would shape human thought for millennia to come.

The alternative interpretation of Genesis, when viewed alongside the Sumerian and Akkadian accounts, presents a cohesive narrative of how displaced nomadic shamans—the Anunnaki—brought their advanced knowledge to early human societies. This perspective sheds new light on the origins of agriculture, settled societies, and the foundations of human civilization. In this reimagined history, Mount Hermon stands not just as a geographical feature, but as a symbol of the meeting point between the celestial knowledge of the Anunnaki and the earthly realm of early humans. Kharsag, far from being a mythical paradise, emerges as a carefully planned agricultural settlement that served as a model for future human societies.

This infusion of knowledge and technology, including the use of the poppy and other medicinal plants, elevated the status of these migrants in the eyes of the Ubaid people, who perceived them as possessing divine wisdom and supernatural abilities. The myths that later emerged in Sumerian culture, particularly those involving the Anunnaki, reflect this perception. The Anunnaki may then be understood to represent these highland migrants who were deified by the indigenous population due to their advanced capabilities. (Remember, though, this is different from the Apkallu beings. These were distinctly described as being semi-biological and not human.

The Sumerian *Atra-Hasis* epic, with its themes of divine beings shaping human destiny, likely encapsulates the collective memory of this significant cultural and technological infusion. The story of the Anunnaki creating humans from clay and their subsequent displeasure with human overpopulation could symbolically represent the highland migrants' role in transforming the agricultural landscape and increasing the population through improved farming techniques. Moreover, the Anunnaki's narrative of descending from the mountains aligns with the historical migration over the Zagros Mountains. This journey was mythologized over generations, transforming the practical reality of migration and cultural exchange into a divine saga. The advanced agricultural and metallurgical knowledge of the highland migrants enabled them to organize and sustain larger, more complex communities, laying the groundwork for what would become the highly advanced Sumerian civilization. In this hypothesis, the Anunnaki are not extraterrestrial beings but rather the highly skilled priest-class who survived the Younger Dryas climatic upheaval. The Apkallu, are their divine celestial sages who can be accessed through secret shamanistic rituals that include psychedelic plants, including the poppy. These otherworldly beings could bestow wisdom, technology, and inspiration through their anointing.

In response to the overwhelming loss of material culture, our survivors of a great cataclysm surely developed a heightened focus on oral tradition, mobility, and the transmission of knowledge. In a world where material possessions could be easily lost to fire, flood, or the ravages of time, the mind became the ultimate repository of knowledge. The devastation survivors of this cataclysm had witnessed instilled in them a deep reverence for the past, manifesting in practices of ancestor worship and a compulsion to expand and explore. Tradition became sacred and protected at all cost. The word *trade* evolved from the idea of walking a path along which goods were exchanged. It comes from the Old English *tredan* ("to tread, step, walk"), which is linked to the PIE root *trehd-* or *tred-* (meaning "to tread, step, or walk"). This root gave rise to words related to walking or stepping in various Indo-European languages. *Tradition*, then, in many ways, can be seen as a journey, much like the well-worn paths of ancient traders who exchanged goods and ideas across vast distances. Just as trade involves the movement of valuable commodities from one place to another, traditions are the cultural treasures passed down through generations, evolving as they traverse the sands of time. This exchange of knowledge, beliefs, and customs is not unlike the barter of goods, where each generation "trades" its wisdom and practices with the next, ensuring their survival and adaptation. As traders shaped the world by bringing diverse cultures into contact, traditions too are shaped by the journeys they undertake, continuously transforming as they encounter new contexts and challenges.

In this way, the act of tradition is inherently linked to the ideas of walking and trading, reflecting the dynamic and evolving nature of cultural heritage. Their migration from the highlands to the fertile plains of Mesopotamia brought significant advancements that were essential in the development of early urban centers, sophisticated agriculture, and social structures. Our ancestors understood that the only way to ensure the survival of their culture was to internalize it, to make it a part of their very being. This is why they developed complex systems of oral tradition, where stories, myths, and rituals were passed down from generation to generation through spoken word and song. Their spirit, once tethered to physical artifacts and familiar landscapes, found its anchor in the intangible realms of religion, ritual, and artistic expression. The profound impact of the arrival and integration of the survivors of this great cataclysm into local cultures was immortalized in myth and the arts, particularly a special type of narrative storytelling based on oral tradition and music.

Preservation of Knowledge: A Response to Trauma

Music is the universal language and is not just an art form but a fundamental aspect of human cognition—one that connects us to our past and helps define our cultural identity. This connection between music, memory, and identity can also be seen in the way young people form deep emotional bonds with the music they encounter during their formative years, typically between the ages of sixteen and twenty-four. This period, when individuals are particularly focused on belonging to a social group or "tribe," is when musical preferences are most strongly established. The songs from this time often become lifelong favorites, anchoring the individual to their past and to their cultural group. In this way, music serves as a powerful tool for creating and maintaining social bonds, much as it did in ancient times.

Music played a particularly vital role in this process. Cognitive studies have shown that music is uniquely capable of remaining in the mind long after other memories have faded. This is evident in cases of Alzheimer's and dementia, where patients may forget who they are but can still remember how to sing or play music. It speaks to its fundamental role in our species' survival strategy.

Steven Pinker's assertion that music is merely "auditory cheesecake"—a byproduct of other cognitive functions—fails to account for the profound importance of music in human culture (Pinker, 1997). While music may be vestigial in some sense, it is also vital, serving as a tool for preserving and transmitting knowledge across generations. The intense focus on music and belonging observed in young people is not merely a quirk of adolescence, but an echo of our ancestors' desperate need to preserve their cultural identity in the face of catastrophic loss. The "song of my people" is quite literally the thread that binds generations across the chasms of time and disaster.

The rhythmic structure of the Sumerians' *Epic of Gilgamesh* and the Greeks' Homeric texts was not a stylistic choice but a mnemonic necessity, allowing vast cultural narratives to be stored in the collective memory of a traumatized species. The distinction between story and epic poetry, and later lyric poetry (derived from the word *lyre*), reflects the evolution of this oral tradition. This oral-musical tradition allowed ancient texts and stories to predate their written forms by centuries or even millennia. Dating flood stories, creation myths, and other ancient accounts solely by the age of the tablets they're written on is thus a fundamentally flawed approach. This is the power of the musical mnemonic, a tool our ancestors used to ensure their history and wisdom could survive future calamities.

The *Epic of Gilgamesh* was not meant to be read in the way we read books today. It was meant to be sung, performed, and remembered. The rhythm of the verse, the repetition of key phrases, and the use of musical accompaniment made it easier for people to recall and transmit these stories. If I were to ask you to recite your favorite book line by line, you would likely find it impossible. But if I asked you to sing the lyrics of your favorite songs, you could probably do so without hesitation. This is the power of music and oral tradition—it embeds knowledge in a way that transcends the limitations of the written word. Today, we often take for granted the written word, seeing it as the ultimate repository of knowledge, but ancient people knew that material objects could be destroyed, and so they turned inward, creating a magical religion that could be transmitted in perpetuity.

The myths and rituals of ancient Mesopotamia were not isolated fragments of history but part of a larger, coherent tradition that has been passed down through the ages, often in forms that we are only now beginning to recognize and understand. In the end, the story of the Sumerians, the Kura-Araxes culture, and the other ancient peoples of the Holocene is not just a story of migration, conquest, and the rise of civilization. It is a story of survival, of the resilience of the human spirit, and of the power of memory, music, and myth to transcend time and space, carrying the wisdom of the past into the present and the future. This is quite literally, *magic*.

CHAPTER 5

POWER OF THE ANUNNAKI

Occult Societies, Bloodlines, and the Tablet of Destinies

The secrets of the gods are not for all men,
but only for those who seek them.

—AESCHYLUS

The café was buzzing with the energy of a warm summer morning, the sunlight streaming through the large windows and casting a golden glow across the room. The place was packed with people—entrepreneurs huddled over laptops, freelancers discussing projects, and the usual crowd of regulars lost in their routines.

I fumbled awkwardly with my bag as I squeezed through the narrow aisle, trying not to knock into anyone's table as I made my way to a table in the back. I tugged at the strap of my bag absentmindedly, hoping it gave off more of a "charmingly disheveled academic" vibe than "overdressed and out of place." I pushed a few stray strands of hair behind my ear, hoping to appear more composed than I felt, but I knew that no matter how put together I may be, my hair always tells a different story. The truth is, I always feel a bit out of my depth in these kinds of settings—surrounded by people who seemed so put together, so confident in their worlds of startups and business deals. Meanwhile, on this day, I was just trying to navigate the strange and shadowy realms that my research had dragged me into.

My friend and colleague Mike Ricksecker arrived shortly after, his entrance marked by a quiet confidence. He spotted me instantly.

"Busy morning," he remarked, his voice carrying just enough above the chatter to reach me. We got our coffee and made our way to a table.

"Mike," I began, trying to steady my voice, "I've been digging deeper into the connections I told you about, and it's getting . . . unsettling. The world of geopolitics is far more intertwined with the occult than I ever imagined. Intelligence agencies, secret societies—they're not just tangentially connected. They're deeply involved in esoteric practices, rituals that are about more than just symbolism. They're trying to claim something—something powerful."

Mike's eyes were sharp as he listened, holding his freshly brewed mocha. "Go on."

I hesitated for a moment, unsure of how to continue. Mike was a fellow researcher who knew the depths of the rabbit hole and who also appeared to be on a quest for truth. I felt that, like mine, his motivation came from a place of genuinely wanting to understand and help others. That's why I called for an in-person meeting. I needed to see his reaction, to gauge whether he thought I was losing my grip on reality.

There was another reason, too—one I couldn't bring myself to mention in that moment. A researcher, someone who had been conversing with the same sources as me, had been found hanged in her garage some months before. The circumstances surrounding her death were suspicious, and rumors of foul play had already begun circulating among those of us who knew her work. While I cannot discuss specific incidents, the intersection of ancient knowledge with modern power structures remains as complex today as it was in ancient Mesopotamia. This is why I approach these topics with both scholarly rigor and appropriate caution.

I had only just learned about the incident, after wondering why I hadn't seen or heard from her in a while, so the news had shaken me. This, in addition to recent exchanges I had with intelligence sources through an encrypted messaging app, made it so I couldn't shake the feeling that I was being watched, that someone or something was keeping tabs on my every move. I needed to talk to Mike in person, away from the prying eyes and ears that might be monitoring our communications. He had worked at the NSA and has had experience when it comes to issues of national security, so I thought maybe he could provide an alternative perspective.

"I've been having conversations with people," I continued, lowering my voice as the weight of the situation pressed down on me. "People who operate in the shadows. What started as what I thought were innocent exchanges turned into something else entirely. I was invited to events that were out of a Stanley Kubrick's *Eyes Wide Shut*-style film. These were parties in medieval castles complete with rituals that I once thought were the stuff of conspiracy theories, but they're real, Mike. These people aren't just LARPing—they're powerbrokers practicing magic in the truest sense of the word. Their rituals aren't just for show; they're about exerting influence, claiming divine rights, and solidifying their power through ancient bloodlines and even genetic research."

Mike leaned in; his focus unwavering. If he thought I was crazy, he was hiding it well.

"It's not as clear-cut as it seems," I continued. "Not all of these people are malevolent. Some are working to counterbalance the darker forces, what you might call 'white hats.' But they're all dangerous in their own ways. I'm walking a tightrope here, trying to understand their true motives without getting pulled in too deep."

"And the Tablet of Destinies?" he asked.

"I think it's central to all of this," I replied, leaning slightly closer as if the very walls might be listening. "Some are in a race to find it. Each faction believes it holds the ultimate secret to life and power, and whoever controls it would have an unassailable claim to rule. It's more than just a relic, mythic or not—it's the key to everything."

We continued to converse, the bustle of the café around us seeming distant and insignificant compared to the gravity of our conversation. I showed him a few of my hastily compiled documents, as we finished our coffee and prepared to leave. I couldn't shake the feeling that this was only the beginning—that what I was uncovering would change everything I thought I knew about history, power, and the unseen forces that shape our world.

Later, I apologized for just laying all of that on him, but his response couldn't have rung more true.

"There are certainly multiple layers of the illusion," he said, his tone both grave and understanding. I couldn't help but wonder how much he might already know. Maybe I had showed my hand too soon. Only later did I wonder whether I'd walked into someone else's script all along.

The implications of what we had discussed continued to weigh heavily on my mind. The depth of the connections between the occult and the powerful forces at play was becoming clearer with each passing day. It wasn't just about the rituals or the hidden meetings—it was about something far deeper, something that had been woven into the very fabric of human history.

Yet, as I continued my research, I couldn't ignore the internal conflict gnawing at me—a moral conundrum that was becoming increasingly difficult to navigate. My Achilles' heel had always been my insatiable curiosity, my almost romantic yearning to know the truth at any cost. There were times when I caught myself being a bit too starry-eyed, perhaps even naive, about the realities I was uncovering. I found myself torn between the allure of diving headfirst into the mysteries that beckoned me and the fear of what might happen if I ventured too far. How close could I get to the edge before I was in too deep? What price was I willing to pay to acquire gnosis?

Part of me longed to retreat, to turn away from these dark and convoluted truths, to focus on writing the fun, intriguing books about ancient astronauts buzzing around pyramids in their spaceships—the kind of stories that had drawn me into this world in the first place (perhaps the sort of story you hoped to find when you picked up this book). Yet, as much as I tried to convince myself that this was enough, the deeper truths kept calling. What I can tell you for sure is that the Anunnaki revelation can be found where the lines between myth and reality, power and magic blurred in unsettling ways. Magic, in the occult sense, is not about illusion but about transformation. It is the ability to tap into the unseen currents that flow through all things, to bend those currents to one's intent. This kind of magic is an ancient practice, rooted in the belief that we live in a "connected universe," as Mike would say.

Thought, word, and action can shape the world in profound ways. Understanding magic in this way reframes it from a simple parlor trick to a powerful tool for shaping reality. It becomes clear why those in positions of power would seek to harness such a force, and why the true nature of magic has been obscured, hidden from the masses and reserved for those initiated into its mysteries. The great magician, Eliphas Levi, in his work *Transcendental Magic: Its Doctrine and Ritual*, encapsulates the essence of occultism:

> *Behind the veil of all heretic and mystical allegories of ancient doctrines, behind the darkness and strange ordeals of all initiations, under the seal of all sacred writings, in the ruins of Nineveh or Thebes, on the crumbling stones of old temples, and on the blackened visage of the Assyrian or Egyptian sphinx, and the monstrous or marvelous paintings which interpret to the faithful of India the inspired pages of the Vedas and the cryptic emblems of our old books on alchemy, and the ceremonies practiced at reception by all secret societies, there are found indications of a doctrine which is everywhere the same and everywhere carefully concealed (1896).*

Levi asserts that behind the allegories, mysteries, and rituals of ancient traditions lies a singular, concealed doctrine. The term occult itself means secret, and secret societies have long been the guardians of esoteric interpretations of religious texts and traditions. These interpretations often stand in stark contrast to the more commonly understood versions of these doctrines, which have historically been used as tools for control and oppression, rather than for spiritual enlightenment and liberation.

The Occult Connection

The Sumerians built their world from the whispers of the Apkallu, those mysterious figures who seemed to exist between the divine and the human. They were divinely inspired—not in the pithy way we may think of being inspired today but rather, by something more akin to a possession. As I explained in *Evil Archaeology*, the word *inspire* comes from Latin *inspirare*, meaning to breathe or blow into. The word was originally used to describe a supernatural imparting an idea to someone. These beings weren't merely mythical—at least, not in the way we think of myths today. To the Sumerians, the Apkallu were real, their presence was felt in the rituals that guided everything from agriculture to the reading of the stars. The Sumerians believed these beings carried the wisdom of the gods, knowledge that was too powerful for ordinary mortals. So, they guarded it, passed it down in secret, and made sure it only reached those who were prepared to handle its weight.

As time passed, this ancient knowledge didn't fade away; it transformed and spread. When Babylon rose to power, they took the Sumerians' secret wisdom and made it their own. The priests of Babylon became the new keepers of these mysteries, using them to guide their kings and predict the future. They studied the stars, believing that the Apkallu's wisdom was written in the heavens, a cosmic script that only they could read. This wasn't just about power; it was about maintaining a connection to something much older, something that reached back to the very dawn of human civilization.

The Magi and the Seven Mysteries of the Anunnaki

The Persians, with their vast empire and their own brand of mysticism, whose legendary priests, the Magi (from which we get the word *magic*), absorbed the teachings of the Babylonians, blending them with their own Zoroastrian beliefs. In their hands, the ancient wisdom took on a new form, one that spoke of the eternal battle between light and darkness. At the heart of the Magi's wisdom lay veneration of the sacred flame, an eternal fire that burned unceasingly in their temples. This reverence for fire was no mere ritual; it symbolized the spiritual light that illuminated the path to understanding the cosmos and its divine architects. The Magi, masters of astronomy and astrology, discerned the movements of the heavens, seeking to unravel the secrets of the celestial bodies and their influence on the mortal realm. This is echoed in the biblical narrative of the Christmas story, with the Magi, sometimes called the Three Wise Men, using their knowledge of the signs in the stars to locate and follow the star of Bethlehem, where they would find the Christ child in a manger.

Central to the Magi's understanding were the seven celestial wanderers, the five visible planets—Mercury, Venus, Mars, Jupiter, and Saturn—along with the Sun and Moon. To the Babylonians, these seven heavenly bodies were the physical manifestations of their great gods: Shamash, the Sun; Sin, the Moon; Nebo, Mercury; Ishtar, Venus; Nergal, Mars; Marduk, Jupiter; and Ea, Saturn. The early Christians and Jews, too, recognized their significance, associating them with the seven archangels and the seven-branched candelabra known as the Temple menorah. The seven wanderers' influence extended far beyond the confines of religion and mythology. They shaped the very fabric of time itself, lending their names to the days of the week in a tradition that endures to this day. The astrological and occult significance of these planetary deities hints at a profound truth: The Anunnaki's power has been in the background of human existence, guiding the cycles of nature and the destiny of civilizations. The universality of the seven and their associated deities across cultures and traditions suggests a shared source of ancient wisdom, a primordial understanding of the cosmos that was imparted to humanity by the Anunnaki themselves.

The Magi's keen observations of the heavens led them to discern the great cycle known as the precession of the equinoxes, a vast celestial dance spanning 25,920 years. This "Great Year" was divided into twelve segments, each corresponding to a zodiacal age lasting roughly 2,160 years. As the Sun's position at the equinox shifted backward through the zodiac, the Magi perceived a profound connection between the changing ages and the rise and fall of civilizations. In this grand cosmic drama, the Anunnaki played the roles of celestial directors, their influence shaping the course of human history. The ancient stargazers of Babylon, perched atop their towering ziggurats, were both astronomers and priests, recognizing no distinction between science and religion. They understood that the movements of the heavens held the key to comprehending the will of the gods and the unfolding of earthly events.

Nibiru

Nibiru, as popularized by modern interpretations, has often been misunderstood to be a mysterious planet beyond Pluto and a harbinger of cataclysmic events, or even the home of the Anunnaki. However, a careful examination of ancient Mesopotamian cuneiform texts and astronomical records reveals a very different, more nuanced understanding of Nibiru. In ancient Mesopotamian cosmology, Nibiru is not a distant, elusive planet, but rather a sophisticated concept deeply rooted in the movements of the planet Jupiter, specifically in its celestial position at its zenith, as the Mesopotamian priest tracked the movement of celestial bodies and their meanings.

The ancient Sumerians and Akkadians, whose astronomical knowledge was both advanced and methodical, recognized Jupiter as one of the five visible planets, referring to it as *Neberu* in Akkadian (Kasak and Veede, 2001). This term is linguistically linked to Nibiru, which is often described in the texts as a celestial body that "divides the sky in half and stands there" (Heiser, n.d., 3). This description is not of a rogue planet but of Jupiter at its zenith—the highest point in the night sky. It is at this point that Jupiter, under the guise of Nibiru, was believed to hold immense astrological significance.

In the MUL.APIN tablets, a cornerstone of Mesopotamian astronomical knowledge, Nibiru is explicitly associated with Jupiter. One of the texts states: "When the stars of Enlil have been finished, one big star—although its light is dim—divides the sky in half and stands there: that is, the star of Marduk, Nibiru, Jupiter; it keeps changing its position and crosses the sky" (Heiser, n.d.). This passage is crucial as it clarifies that Nibiru is not an anomalous planet but rather Jupiter at its zenith, a moment of cosmic balance and power.

The association of Nibiru with Marduk, the chief deity of Babylon, further cements its importance in Mesopotamian religion and astrology. Marduk, who rose to prominence in the Babylonian pantheon, was often equated with Jupiter (Sommerfield, 1982). This connection is evident in the way Nibiru is described as the "star of Marduk," a celestial manifestation of the god's authority and influence (Lambert, 1984). As Marduk was seen as the deity who brought order out of chaos, Jupiter's position at the zenith—symbolizing the highest point of order and stability in the sky—became synonymous with Nibiru.

This interpretation of Nibiru as Jupiter's zenith position offers a new perspective on the planet's role in both ancient and modern esoteric traditions. In Mesopotamian astrology, the moment when Jupiter reached its zenith was considered a time of immense power, associated with prosperity, kingship, and divine favor. Tablet No. 187 from the British Museum collection, translated by R. Campbell Thompson in *The Reports of the Magicians and Astrologers of Nineveh and Babylon*, provides a clear example: "When Jupiter (Sagmigar) assumes a brilliance in the tropic of Cancer and becomes Nibiru, Akkad will overflow with plenty, the king of Akkad will grow powerful" (Thompson, 1900). This text links the zenith of Jupiter with abundance and the strength of kingship, concepts central to both magical practice and governance in ancient Mesopotamia.

Furthermore, another passage from the same collection, Tablet No. 94, expands on the astrological importance of Jupiter's zenith: "When a halo surrounds the Moon and Jupiter (Nibiru) stands within it, there will be a slaughter of cattle and beasts of the field. (Marduk is Umunpauddu at its appearance; when it has risen for two [or four?] hours it becomes Sagmigar; when it stands in the meridian it becomes Nibiru)" (Thompson, 1900). This description directly equates Nibiru with Jupiter when it stands at the meridian, or zenith, further reinforcing that Nibiru is not a separate celestial body but a specific position of Jupiter.

The implications of this interpretation extend beyond the historical and into the esoteric. The daily ascent of Jupiter to its zenith, recognized as Nibiru, can be seen as an allegory for spiritual ascension in Western esoteric traditions. The hermetic principle "As above, so below" finds a literal expression in this celestial phenomenon, where Jupiter's zenith represents a moment of perfect balance and maximum potential—a cosmic reflection of the magician's quest for spiritual elevation (Needham, 1980).

This concept aligns closely with the alchemical Great Work, where base matter is transmuted into the philosopher's stone. In this context, Jupiter's transformation into Nibiru at its zenith symbolizes this alchemical process, marking a brief window where celestial and terrestrial realms converge, facilitating potent magical operations. For contemporary practitioners of ceremonial magic, understanding Nibiru as Jupiter's zenith offers a powerful tool for ritual timing. By aligning magical workings with Jupiter's daily Nibiru, practitioners attempt to harness celestial influences for the manifestation of abundance, power, and spiritual growth.

The principle articulated in the *Emerald Tablet of Hermes Trismegistus*—"That which is below is like that which is above & that which is above is like that which is below to do the miracles of one only thing"—is beautifully exemplified in the concept of Nibiru as Jupiter's zenith. It is a moment when the divine order established by Marduk in the heavens is mirrored in the workings of the earth, offering an opportunity for those attuned to these celestial rhythms to access profound spiritual insights and transformative power (Needham, 1980). Moreover, the concept of Nibiru as Jupiter's zenith resonates with broader esoteric cosmologies that emphasize the cyclical nature of time and the universe. It mirrors the cyclical nature found in various traditions, from the Hindu Yugas to Hesiod's Ages of Man. Each daily ascent of Jupiter to Nibiru serves as a microcosm of larger celestial cycles, embodying the eternal rhythm of ascent and descent, of golden ages and dark ages, played out on a cosmic scale. This perspective illustrates that opportunities for transformation and enlightenment occur not through rare cosmic alignments but through daily celestial events accessible to the discerning observer.

This understanding of Nibiru, grounded in the astronomical and theological traditions of ancient Mesopotamia, also allows for a more nuanced interpretation of the historical records. The Mesopotamian cuneiform record repeatedly describes Nibiru in ways that align with this view, consistently identifying it with Jupiter and never with a planet beyond Pluto. The ancient

Mesopotamians were aware of five visible planets—Mercury, Venus, Mars, Jupiter, and Saturn—and this understanding is clearly outlined in the MUL.APIN tablets and other astronomical texts (Kasak and Veede, 2001).

Recognizing Nibiru as Jupiter's daily zenith restores the concept to its rightful place in the cosmic order. It represents not a distant, foreboding planet but a recurring moment of power and potential within the celestial dance. This understanding bridges ancient astronomical observations with esoteric practice, offering a framework for exploring cosmic influences on terrestrial affairs. In the context of esoteric traditions, Marduk's association with Jupiter and the identification of Nibiru as Jupiter's zenith can be seen as a reflection of the divine authority and order that Marduk embodies. As Marduk was the god who defeated chaos and established order in the universe, so too does Jupiter's zenith represent a moment of cosmic stability and alignment, a time when the divine order is most potent. This alignment with Marduk's mythos offers a profound symbol for the esoteric practitioner, who seeks to harness the powers of order and stability in their own spiritual journey.

Marduk's rise to prominence in the Babylonian pantheon, paralleled by Jupiter's ascent to its zenith, can be seen as a metaphor for the spiritual path of ascension. Just as Marduk ascended to the position of king of the gods, bringing order to the cosmos, so too does the esoteric practitioner seek to rise to a position of spiritual authority, bringing order to the chaos within. This ascent is mirrored in the daily movement of Jupiter as it rises to its zenith, a moment that offers a powerful opportunity for spiritual growth and transformation (Lambert, 1984).

This cyclical pattern of rise and fall, of order emerging from chaos and then returning to it, is a central theme in many esoteric traditions. In the daily rise of Jupiter to Nibiru, we see a reflection of this eternal cycle, a reminder that the forces of order and chaos are in constant interplay, both in the cosmos and within ourselves. By aligning with this cosmic rhythm, the practitioner can tap into the deeper currents of the universe, accessing the wisdom and power that comes from being in harmony with the celestial order. Jupiter's daily zenith, the moment of Nibiru's "passing over," is a celestial phenomenon seen as the veil, then referred to as "the firmament" between humans and the beings from beyond, who could lead them through the complexities of the cosmos.

Seeing Beyond the Firmament

As Persian influence spread, so did this secret knowledge, winding its way into Egypt and Greece. In the mystery schools of these lands, the teachings of the Apkallu reappeared, though now dressed in the symbols and languages of new cultures. The Greeks, always eager to learn from others, fused this wisdom with their own philosophy, creating something that felt both ancient and entirely new. These were the seeds of Hermeticism, a tradition that promised hidden truths and direct encounters with the divine. The Apkallu had transformed once again, now seen as spiritual guides within the mysteries that sought to transcend the limits of the human mind.

This ancient thread continued through the rise of Christianity, where it took on yet another form. The early Gnostics, often marginalized and persecuted, found in these old teachings a source of strength and insight. They spoke of hidden knowledge, of archons and otherworldly beings who controlled the material world. For the Gnostics, the path to salvation was through secret wisdom, a knowledge that would allow them to break free from the physical realm and reconnect with the divine. The Apkallu, now nearly unrecognizable, were still there in the background, their essence woven into the fabric of Gnostic thought.

When the Islamic world became the new center of learning, this knowledge was preserved and expanded. The scholars of the Islamic Golden Age translated and studied the ancient texts, ensuring that the wisdom of the Apkallu would not be lost. Sufi mystics in particular embraced these teachings, seeking personal encounters with the divine through their spiritual practices. The idea of communing with otherworldly beings remained, though now framed within a different religious context. The Sufis, like the mystics before them, believed that true understanding came from these direct encounters, experiences that connected them to a lineage stretching back to the dawn of history.

Renaissance Secret Societies

By the time this knowledge returned to Europe, it had been transformed so many times that its origins were almost forgotten. Yet, in the monasteries and secret societies of medieval Europe, the flame of this ancient wisdom still burned. The alchemists, Kabbalists, and Christian mystics of this period were all searching for something more, something that lay beyond the reach of ordinary religion. They sought to contact higher beings, to access a knowledge that had been passed down through the ages, a knowledge that still carried the imprint of the Apkallu.

The Renaissance brought a renewed interest in these ancient teachings, sparking a revival of Hermeticism and other esoteric traditions. Scholars and magicians of the time rediscovered the old texts and began to piece together the lineage of knowledge that connected them to the distant past. They believed that through their studies and rituals, they could tap into the same source of wisdom that the Sumerians had once revered. The Apkallu, though transformed beyond recognition, still influenced these seekers, guiding them in their quest for hidden truths.

Thus, as the early modern era approached, this ancient thread continued to weave its way through history, shaping the thoughts and beliefs of those who were drawn to the mysteries. Secret societies like the Freemasons and the Rosicrucians took up the mantle, claiming to preserve a knowledge that was as old as civilization itself. The idea of communing with discarnate entities, of seeking wisdom from beyond the human realm, remained a constant, a thread that tied together all these disparate traditions.

In each era, in each transformation, the essence of that ancient Sumerian wisdom endured. The Apkallu might have changed names and forms, but their presence was still felt, guiding those who sought to understand the deeper truths of the world. From the ziggurats of Sumer to the secret lodges of the Illuminati, the knowledge of the Apkallu has persisted, a hidden lineage of wisdom that has shaped the course of history.

Hidden Hands

The Apkallu entities that the Anunnaki shamans contacted represent archetypal forces that manifest through human consciousness. The Anunnaki themselves were the human practitioners who developed the rituals and symbols, like the poppy rosettes, to facilitate contact with these otherworldly Apkallu beings. This idea is not new, of course. King Solomon stands out as a legendary exemplar of such power. Solomon, renowned for his wisdom, is traditionally associated with magical and esoteric knowledge. The Testament of Solomon, a pseudepigraphical work, portrays him as knowing how to summon and control otherworldly beings using his magical seal. His possession of Solomon's Key made him one of the most powerful kings in history, not merely because of his wealth or wisdom, but because of his mastery over forces beyond the physical world. "And I Solomon questioned him, saying, 'Who art thou?' And he replied, 'I am called Ornias, and I hover about the firmament of heaven" (Conybeare, 1898). Pablo A. Torijano, in his analysis of Solomon traditions, argues that the figure of Solomon as a magician and exorcist had a profound impact on later magical and esoteric traditions. He notes, "The image of Solomon as master over demons and possessor of occult knowledge became a powerful archetype in Jewish, Christian, and Islamic magical traditions" (Torijano, 2002).

In much the same way, the Anunnaki are perceived within some occult circles as entities that can be summoned and directed through precise rituals and knowledge. These rituals are not just relics of an ancient past; they are seen as living traditions, practices that have been preserved and passed down through mystery schools, occult societies, and secret orders. For these groups, the Anunnaki are not merely symbolic figures, but tangible forces of power that, if properly harnessed, could grant unparalleled authority over both the material and spiritual realms.

The rituals associated with these powerful entities often involve elaborate ceremonies, symbols, and the invocation of specific names or words of power. In the case of the Anunnaki, these rituals might include the recitation of ancient Sumerian hymns, the use of sigils associated with the Anunnaki gods, or the creation of sacred spaces designed to resonate with the energies of these entities. The goal of these rituals is to establish a connection with the Anunnaki, to draw upon their power, and to direct that power towards specific ends—whether those ends are personal, political, or spiritual.

Secret societies and occult organizations have long understood the importance of these rituals and the power they can confer. Groups such as the Freemasons, the Rosicrucians, and the Illuminati have been rumored to incorporate elements of Anunnaki lore into their practices, seeing in these ancient entities a source of wisdom and power that can be used to influence the course of history. These societies often cloak their rituals in secrecy, aware that the knowledge they possess, if it were to become widely known, could disrupt the balance of power in the world.

The Divine Right of Kings and Occult Bloodlines

The idea that the Anunnaki could be invoked to grant power and influence is not limited to the realm of the occult. Rulers and elites have sought out methods to legitimize and consolidate their power, often turning to the divine or the supernatural for support. The concept of the divine right of kings, for example, is rooted in the belief that rulers are chosen by the gods and endowed with a special connection to the divine. In the case of the Anunnaki, this connection is seen as a direct link to the ancient gods who shaped human civilization, a link that can be reactivated through the correct rituals and practices.

In *The Histories* (4.8–10), Herodotus recounts a fascinating legend that claims all Scythians descended from Hercules and a mysterious serpent-woman hybrid, echoing later European folklore. This serpentine figure bears a striking resemblance to Melusine, a prominent figure in European folklore, particularly in French and German legends. Melusine, born to a human king and a fairy, was cursed to transform into a serpent from the waist down every Saturday. Her tale, famously recorded by Jean d'Arras in the fourteenth century, touches on themes of transformation, supernatural worlds, and broken vows.

Melusine's story begins with her mother's flight to Avalon after her father's broken promise. In revenge, Melusine imprisoned her father, leading to her mother's curse. She later married a nobleman, Raymondin, with the condition that he never see her on Saturdays. Inevitably, curiosity led him to discover her secret, causing Melusine to depart, though she continued to watch over her descendants.

The legend of Melusine is deeply intertwined with European nobility and aristocracy, particularly the Lusignan family of France. Her image was adopted in their heraldry, and she's credited with founding several castles and churches across Europe. The tale has left a lasting impact on art, literature, and even modern branding—the Starbucks logo is often said to be inspired by Melusine, though the company describes it as a twin-tailed siren.

Melusine's legend shares similarities with other mythological figures like the Mesopotamian Oannes, the god Enki, and Nammu, the primordial sea goddess and mother of Enki. These beings, often depicted as half-human and half-aquatic, symbolize the intersection of human and divine realms. Like Melusine, they are deeply connected to water, which serves as a symbol of life, mystery, and transformation in many mythologies. Oannes, from Sumerian and Babylonian mythology, is often depicted as a half-man, half-fish being who emerged from the sea to bring knowledge to humanity. Similarly, Enki is often symbolized as half-fish. These hybrid forms, combining human and aquatic features, may represent the blending of different realms or the idea of beings who traverse the boundary between the human and the divine. Additionally, in esoteric interpretations, these figures represent archetypal symbols of hidden knowledge and the mysteries of existence. Melusine's secret serpent form and

Oannes's emergence from the depths of the sea could represent hidden truths or the dual nature of reality—seen and unseen, known and unknown. They are bearers or guardians of knowledge, embodying the tension between the human and supernatural worlds.

Melusine, *newly printed in Paris by Michel Le Noir, 1517. This illustration depicts Melusine, a legendary figure from European folklore, often portrayed as a mermaid or serpent-like woman. The print showcases the artistic style of early sixteenth-century France.*

The Merovingian Dynasty and the Divine Bloodline

The Merovingian dynasty, ruling the Franks from the fifth to eighth centuries, traces its origins to the semi-mythical figure Mérovée. Legend claims he was born of two fathers: King Clodio and a "beast of Neptune" or Quinotaur. This dual parentage suggests a connection to otherworldly beings, which some modern elites interpret as a link to the ancient Mesopotamian Apkallu or Oannes. The Merovingians were known as "long-haired kings" and believed to possess supernatural powers. They were seen as priest-kings, embodying divine grace similar to ancient Egyptian pharaohs, and their aura of magic and esoteric knowledge was central to their identity. The discovery of King Childeric I's tomb, filled with magical and ritualistic items, including gold bees and a crystal ball, highlights the dynasty's enduring link to sorcery and the supernatural. Such artifacts were believed to embody the Merovingians' spiritual authority.

Lawrence Gardner (1996) explores these legends, suggesting that the Merovingians' claim to divine bloodlines may be rooted in ancient traditions. Some modern elites, viewing themselves as inheritors of this sacred lineage, see their supposed connection to the Oannes/Apkallu as a source of their right to rule and supernatural authority. Recent genetic studies provide intriguing insights into the origins of these ancient peoples, as we saw in the previous chapter. A 2017 study suggested a connection between the Scythians and the earlier Yamnaya culture, known for its red ochre burial traditions dating back to 3300 BC (Unterländer et al., 2017). This link bridges Bronze Age steppe cultures with later Indo-European groups that dominated much of Eurasia.

The terms *Saka* and *Scythian* were often used interchangeably in ancient sources. Herodotus noted that Persians called all Scythians "Saka." Some historians speculate that the Scythians were among the Ten Lost Tribes of Israel, allied with the Phoenician Empire (Koestler, 1976). This connection to sacred bloodlines extends to Greek mythology, where Japheth's lineage is linked to the Greek Titan Iapetus, mentioned by Homer in the *Iliad* as the ancestor of the Hellenic people. The Merovingian dynasty, ruling the Franks from the fifth century until 751, was also considered part of this ancient noble lineage.

These interconnected myths and legends span from the steppes of Central Asia to the courts of medieval Europe but have links right back to Mesopotamia. The Merovingians' claim to divine bloodlines may not be entirely symbolic but rooted in an ancient tradition that these elites, who believe themselves to be of royal blood, interpret as a connection to the Apkallu—a belief system that continues to influence their perceptions of power and legitimacy. These elites, viewing themselves as inheritors of this sacred bloodline, consider their connection to the Oannes/Apkallu as a source of their right to rule, imbued with the wisdom and supernatural authority passed down from these ancient beings.

The Magdalene Lineage and the Sacred Marriage

Whether through symbolic lineage or actual belief in their divine heritage, the legend of the Merovingians continues to resonate with those who see themselves as the modern-day bearers of this ancient and mystical legacy, including those who consider themselves the descendants of Jesus Christ and Mary Magdalene. Even the title, not surname, Magdalene, linked to the word *whorelet*, comes from the ancient and obscure word *hierodule*, which can be traced back to the Sumerian "Song of Inanna" from around 2500 BC (Gardner, 1996). This erotic hymn, related to the sacred marriage of the goddess Inanna and the shepherd Dumuzi (also known as Tammuz, for whom the women of Israel wept as mentioned in Ezekiel 8:14), is significant. In those times, kings were referred to as "Shepherds," symbolizing their role as guardians of their flocks, with the goddess Inanna (or Ishtar) acting as the "Magdal-eder," the Watchtower of the flock, presiding from the Great House of the E-gal. This is where the title Magdalene originates. Notably, when Mary is introduced in Luke 8:2, she is referred to as "Mary called Magdalene," indicating her status rather than a surname or geographic origin (Gardner, 1996).

In Mesopotamian Sumer, the land of Abraham, as mentioned in Genesis 11:28–31, the priest-king was known as the *Sanga-lugal*, a term from which the French word *sang* ("blood," as in "Sangreal" or "Blood Royal") is derived (Gardner, 1996). His symbol of authority was a shepherd's staff, or crook, which later became misappropriated by the Christian Church as an instrument of authority for bishops. The goddess Inanna was revered as the "cup-bearer," whose sacred essence, called the *Gra-al* (later known as the Grail), symbolized the "nectar of supreme excellence" (Gardner, 1996,143). The concept of the Holy Grail, often associated with the cup used by Jesus at the Last Supper, actually predates Christianity and is deeply rooted in earlier traditions.

In this context, the hierodule, as represented by Inanna, played a central role in the sacred bridal ritual. Inanna, goddess of light and fire, was later equated with Diana of the Nine Fires, with her symbol being the *Rosi-crucis* or Dew Cup, a cross within a circle that became the original emblem of the Holy Grail. The *hierodulai*, plural for hierodule, were sacred women associated with the high priestesses of the Order of Diana of Ephesus during New Testament times. Their robes were red, symbolizing *ritu* ("truth"), which is the root of the word *ritual*. Mary Magdalene is often depicted wearing red in artistic representations, symbolizing her role as a hierodule. However, due to linguistic corruption before the Bible, the term *hierodule* became associated with *harlot*, leading to the conflation of Inanna with the Whore of Babylon in the book of Revelation 17:1–5.

Consequently, the color red became linked to prostitution, a connection that persists in modern imagery, such as the use of red lights in brothels. Despite these distortions, the hierodule was central to the Sacred Marriage, or *hieros gamos*, a ritual that is echoed in the Old Testament Song of Solomon and the New Testament marriage scenes of Jesus and Mary Magdalene (Gardner, 1996, 144).

Rex Deus: The Royal Bloodlines and Ancient Traditions

According to many esoteric traditions, certain bloodlines are believed to carry within them the potential for divine power. These bloodlines are often traced back to ancient rulers or gods and are thought to possess a unique connection to the forces that govern the universe. The Sumerian King List, which chronicles the reigns of ancient Mesopotamian rulers, is not just a historical record but rather a document that encodes the secrets of divine rule, offering clues to the location of the Tablet of Destinies and the knowledge it contains.

This obsession with bloodlines and the pursuit of power through the Anunnaki has deep roots in the history of secret societies. The work of my friend and colleague, the late Tim Wallace-Murphy, on the Rex Deus families explores how certain bloodlines, believed to be descended from the biblical Davidic line, have been linked to the search for ancient knowledge and power. These families, known as *Rex Deus* or "Kings of God," claim to possess a unique connection to the divine, one that grants them access to the hidden knowledge of the universe. Freemasonry, with its roots in the teachings of the Persian Magi and King Solomon, became the foundation for esoteric traditions in Europe. These teachings, associated with the Holy Grail legends, are believed by some to symbolize a particular bloodline—tracing back to the twenty-four high priests of the Temple of Jerusalem, including the family of Jesus. According to some esoteric traditions, Jesus was not only a spiritual leader but also a rabbi and heir to the throne of David, obligated to marry and produce an heir. This belief, long suppressed by the Church, suggests that Jesus founded a bloodline known as the Desposyni, which still exists in Europe today (Hopkins and Wallace-Murphy, 2000). Some descendants of this bloodline may not even be aware of their lineage, living ordinary lives while their heritage remains hidden. This hidden lineage is connected to secret societies and has played a significant role in shaping European culture. The Knights Templar, a Catholic military order founded by these bloodlines, were instrumental in spreading these esoteric teachings, which later influenced the development of Freemasonry. This hidden lineage, connected to secret societies and esoteric traditions, exerted significant influence on European culture and later global cultures, with their influence extending into contemporary times, shaping global events from behind the scenes.

The idea of powerful bloodlines has persisted in modern times with some influential families being part of a broader narrative that ties them to the descendants of the Knights Templar and other esoteric groups, often associated with nationalist ideologies that seek to preserve cultural and genetic identities in the face of global change. In contrast, another faction advocates for the dissolution of traditional power structures and the creation of a borderless, secular society based on Marxist ideologies. This ongoing struggle between preserving ancient bloodlines and embracing a new world order continues to shape contemporary political and social landscapes, echoing the ancient conflicts for global supremacy that some occultists believe originated in the lost city of Atlantis, which they view as not a mythological sunken island, but rather, the location of their Pleistocene utopia where advanced knowledge of technology (magic) flourished as a result of their relationship with the gods. These gods, as we understand it today, were said to have "walked with them" because they had such strong psychokinetic and telepathic connections that their shamans were quite literally conduits for their Great Work in creating mankind.

The influence of these ancient bloodlines is still felt today, with some modern royal families, including the British monarchy, claiming descent from these lineages. The late Queen Elizabeth and King Charles III, for example, can trace their ancestry back to Fatima, the daughter of the Prophet Muhammad, through a lineage that crosses medieval Muslim Spain and the House of David. These connections between ancient bloodlines, royal families, and global power dynamics are reflected in historical events like the Balfour Declaration, which laid the groundwork for the establishment of Israel. The continued influence of Freemasonry and other esoteric traditions suggests that the ancient struggle for power, rooted in the legends of Atlantis and the descendants of the Magi, persists in the modern world, shaping the course of history in ways that are often hidden from public view. These connections are believed to be not only spiritual, but also physical, because as Levi and other occult magicians point out, the power can be found in the blood itself. The belief in a divine mandate tied to ancient bloodlines is not merely a matter of faith, but a practical tool for maintaining control. The belief that certain bloodlines are connected to the Anunnaki grants these families a special status, one that justifies their dominance over others. This idea is not limited to ancient times; it has persisted throughout history and continues to influence modern power structures.

The Tablet of Destinies

The Tablet of Destinies has long been associated with the consolidation of divine authority. In Mesopotamian tradition, it was believed to contain the decrees of the gods, functioning as a sacred record that conferred legitimacy and dominion upon its holder. Among some hidden traditions, this tablet has come to represent more than myth; it signified access to the hidden architecture of fate itself. Within elite circles that trace their lineage to Anunnaki (or were chosen by them), the tablet represents more than myth. It is seen as a literal or symbolic source of control over world events. Hidden traditions later interpreted the Tablet of Destinies as containing the blueprint of fate itself, a sacred object that, in the right hands, could be used to manipulate destiny, preserve dynasties, and secure dominion across generations. The idea that such knowledge could be preserved or retrieved has inspired both literal quests and symbolic rites across time, each rooted in the belief that destiny is not inherited but controlled by those who possess not only the right blood, but the proper key.

The Sumerian understanding of divine order is intrinsically linked to the concept of *me* (pronounced "may"), a term that defies simple translation but encompasses the fundamental, unalterable principles governing all aspects of civilized existence. These *me* principles represent more than mere rules or guidelines; they embody the very essence of civilization and cosmic functionality. These abstract notions materialize in the form of the *Tablet of Destinies*, which is made up of clay tablets imbued with the power to determine the fates of all things. The Tablet of Destinies is first mentioned in the Babylonian creation epic, *Enuma Elish* (Dalley, 2000).

The *me* represent a comprehensive assortment of powers, duties, norms, standards, rules, and regulations that form the bedrock of cosmic and societal function. These are not merely abstract concepts but active forces shaping the fabric of reality. In Sumerian thought, these principles were not created but existed eternally, predating even the gods themselves. The possession and control of the *me* granted supreme authority over the cosmos, making them objects of immense desire and contention among divine beings.

This cylinder seal from the British Museum illustrates the god Enki and the mythological bird Anzu.

In the narrative of the *Enuma Elish*, the tablets initially belong to Tiamat, the primordial goddess of saltwater. After her defeat by Marduk, the tablets pass to him, symbolizing his ascension to supreme godhood. This transfer of the tablets represents more than a mere change of ownership; it signifies a fundamental shift in the cosmic order, a new divine regime taking control of the universe's operating principles.

The power inherent in the Tablet of Destinies extends far beyond mere symbolic authority. It is described as containing the fates of gods and mortals alike, the blueprints of existence itself. To possess the tablet is to hold the power to decree destinies, to shape the very course of cosmic events. This concept reflects a profound understanding of the relationship between knowledge and power, suggesting that ultimate authority stems from comprehension and control of the universe's fundamental laws.

The Sumerian conception of the Tablet of Destinies introduces a crucial element into the narrative of cosmic order: the idea that this divine knowledge and power can be contained, transferred, and potentially manipulated. This notion sets the stage for later mythological and philosophical explorations of humanity's relationship to divine knowledge and our potential to understand and perhaps influence the cosmic order.

Furthermore, the concept of the Tablet of Destinies resonates with later religious and esoteric traditions that speak of sacred texts or objects containing supreme wisdom or power. From the Biblical Ark of the Covenant to the Holy Grail of Arthurian legend, the idea of a physical repository of divine knowledge and power recurs throughout human spiritual and cultural evolution. In the context of the Anunnaki, the Tablet of Destinies becomes more than a literary device—it transforms into a potential key to unlocking the very fabric of reality itself. This belief has driven countless individuals and groups to search for either the literal tablet or the hidden knowledge it supposedly contains.

The Quest for Ultimate Power

The allure of such cosmic power hasn't been limited to the fringes of society. Throughout history, ruling elites have often claimed divine mandate or supernatural authority to legitimize their positions. These claims frequently involve assertions of special bloodlines or inherited spiritual gifts, concepts that align closely with esoteric interpretations of the Anunnaki's influence on human affairs. The Sumerian King List, with its accounts of early rulers reigning for tens of thousands of years, provides a tantalizing link between the mortal world and the realm of the gods (Jacobsen, 1939).

While mainstream historians view these impossibly long reigns as symbolic or exaggerated, some esoteric traditions interpret them as evidence of a time when the Anunnaki walked among humans, bestowing their divine essence upon certain lineages. This idea of divinely ordained bloodlines has persisted in various forms, from the concept of the divine right of kings in European monarchies to more obscure claims of hidden royal lineages preserved by secret societies.

Sumerian King List, 1800 BCE, Larsa, Iraq. This artifact documents the ancient rulers of Sumer in chronological order, offering crucial insights into Mesopotamian history and chronology.

The intersection of these beliefs with political power became starkly apparent during the twentieth century, most notably in the actions of Nazi Germany's Ahnenerbe organization. Under Heinrich Himmler's direction, this group scoured the globe for artifacts believed to hold supernatural power, driven by a mix of pseudohistorical theories and occult beliefs (Pringle, 2006). While their search focused primarily on items from European mythology, the underlying principle—that physical objects or hidden knowledge could grant supreme authority—mirrors the concept of the Tablet of Destinies and other Anunnaki-related lore. This real-world example demonstrates how ancient myths can be reinterpreted and weaponized in the pursuit of political and ideological goals, a pattern that continues to manifest in various forms today.

My research posits that the Anunnaki figures were not divine beings but rather a shamanic elite displaced during the Ice Age. Their migration, possibly from the far east, including regions like Siberia and Mongolia, brought them to Anatolia, where they established early spiritual and architectural traditions at sites such as Karahan Tepe. This idea aligns with growing evidence that points to these ancient peoples as the true architects behind monumental sites, which later civilizations would mythologize as the work of gods.

Central to their spiritual system was the serpent motif, a symbol of cosmic knowledge and transformation. My work has emphasized that this serpent was not merely a metaphor but represented a sophisticated understanding of celestial forces. The Anunnaki's architectural prowess, seen in their use of sacred geometry and cosmic alignments, suggests that they intentionally embedded their astronomical knowledge into the very foundations of their sacred structures. This idea is supported by discoveries at Karahan Tepe, where the serpent features prominently in rock-cut temples believed to have been used for rituals designed to connect with cosmic energies, particularly the Milky Way's galactic bulge and the stars of Scorpius.

These serpent shrines, as I have long argued, were places of oracular communication, where the shamanic elites sought to tap into altered states of consciousness through rituals. The serpent was central to these rites, symbolizing the transformation of the individual and their connection to a higher cosmic order. What's more, this serpent imagery and its associated wisdom persisted long after the Anunnaki's influence, reappearing in later spiritual movements and esoteric traditions. Gnostic sects, such as the Ophites, embraced the serpent as a symbol of divine knowledge, a notion that resonates with the ancient rites practiced at sites like Karahan Tepe.

The vilification of the serpent in later religious texts, such as in the story of the Garden of Eden, was a deliberate inversion of its original significance. Where ancient cultures saw the serpent as a guide to higher knowledge, later traditions recast it as a symbol of deceit and corruption. This shift can be traced to a misunderstanding—or deliberate suppression—of the Anunnaki's shamanic practices and their cosmological teachings. The Anunnaki were not just early builders of civilization; they were custodians of a profound, esoteric knowledge that later societies either lost or intentionally distorted.

The persistence of these ancient traditions into later Gnostic and occult movements reveals the depth of the Anunnaki's legacy. The serpent, long a symbol of wisdom and power, became central to secret societies and spiritual movements that sought to preserve the lost knowledge of the ancient world. This continuity is a testament to the enduring influence of the Anunnaki's esoteric practices, and my research has shown that their knowledge—particularly their use of sacred geometry and celestial alignments—formed the backbone of these later traditions.

Moreover, their architectural and cosmological knowledge wasn't limited to symbolic serpent worship. The Anunnaki were responsible for early advancements in agriculture, such as the domestication of wheat, which took place in the same regions where these monumental sites were constructed. The parallels between these agricultural developments and the establishment of sacred spaces point to a culture deeply embedded in both the practical and the spiritual, a union of earthly and cosmic knowledge.

In tracing these threads from the most recent ice age to the present, it becomes clear that the Anunnaki's legacy is far-reaching. Their impact is not confined to myth but stretches into the spiritual, architectural, and scientific foundations of human civilization. My research continues to reveal how their sacred practices—rooted in shamanic traditions, cosmic alignments, and a deep understanding of the natural world—shaped the esoteric currents that would later reemerge in occult societies and mystical movements across the ages. This lasting legacy, one of knowledge encoded in both the earth and the stars, remains a vital key to understanding the true nature of the Anunnaki and their enduring influence on humanity.

In my quest to understand the Anunnaki and their role in shaping early civilization, I've had the opportunity to collaborate with many researchers and thought leaders who share the same passion for uncovering the past. One such conversation that stands out was with Edmund Marriage, the principal of the Patrick Foundation, who has dedicated his life to continuing the groundbreaking work of Christian and Barbara Joy O'Brien. The O'Briens' research into ancient Sumerian texts, particularly their study of Kharsag, provided some of the clearest evidence that the Anunnaki were not mere mythological beings but historical figures whose contributions to humanity were real and measurable.

As Edmund and I sat down to discuss this groundbreaking work, he conveyed a depth of insight shaped by decades of research and personal connection to the O'Briens' legacy. As principal of the Patrick Foundation, Edmund dedicated himself to continuing their work, and his commitment was evident in every detail he shared.

"You know, Christian's work as an exploration geologist really set the stage for their discoveries," Edmund began. "He and Barbara Joy spent years analyzing the Kharsag tablets, finding that these weren't just myths but actual historical records detailing the presence of the Anunnaki on Earth."

According to the O'Briens' interpretations, the Anunnaki—described in Sumerian texts as "those who came from the heavens"—were not simply deities or archetypes but advanced beings who played an active, constructive role in human development. "The Sumerians saw the Anunnaki not merely as gods but as practical, almost scientific figures," Edmund explained. "They were responsible for teaching early humans critical advancements—how to farm, how to build cities, how to harness natural resources. They were seen as the bringers of knowledge and civilization itself."

Edmund emphasized that Kharsag, which the O'Briens believed to be the Anunnaki's base of operations, was a real place—not a metaphor or spiritual abstraction. "Christian and Barbara Joy believed Kharsag was a place where 'heaven and earth met,' likely in the Zagros Mountains, though early versions of the *Epic of Gilgamesh* had it confused with later references to Lebanon."

The identification of the Zagros Mountains was not arbitrary. Edmund highlighted how Christian's geological background enabled them to connect the location of Kharsag with hard data. "This was a key discovery," he said, "as it aligned with paleoclimatological data showing that around 8500 BC, this region experienced dramatic changes. Monsoons transformed the land into a fertile paradise, which allowed the Anunnaki to establish the first Neolithic communities."

Edmund continued, elaborating on the significance of the cedar forests often mentioned in ancient texts. "The O'Briens originally thought Kharsag might be located in Lebanon due to those references, but as they dug deeper, they found that the oldest versions of the *Epic of Gilgamesh* placed these forests in the Zagros Mountains of Kurdistan. That was a game changer."

This agricultural connection was central to the O'Briens' thesis. "The Anunnaki weren't just passive overseers," Edmund added. "They actively participated in shaping human progress. The rise of agriculture and structured society was seen as a direct result of their teachings."

As we spoke, he also addressed the issue of ecological change over time. "By around 3000 to 2000 BC, these cedar forests began to disappear due to human activity, particularly deforestation. The Sumerians needed the wood for construction and fuel, and this led to a major ecological shift in the region. It also meant that later generations forgot the true location of the Anunnaki's settlement."

Then he brought up Mount Hermon. "Christian initially considered that Kharsag might be linked to Mount Hermon in the Ante-Lebanon range, which some associate with the Book of Enoch. But after more study, he favored the idea that Kharsag lay farther east, likely in the Zagros Mountains."

Edmund's passion for the Anunnaki's legacy was unmistakable. "The Anunnaki weren't just mythological figures to them. Christian and Barbara Joy saw these beings as integral to the story of how human civilization came to be. Their contributions laid the foundation for everything that followed—their legacy is embedded in human history."

As our conversation drew to a close, Edmund reflected with quiet intensity. "Their research truly opened new doors for understanding our ancient past. The Anunnaki weren't just gods—they were the architects of civilization."

As I reflected on our discussion, another line of thinking began to surface—about the Tas Tepeler culture. The discovery of

Tas Tepeler, which translates to "stone hills" in Turkish, is considered revolutionary in the field of archaeology. This ancient culture flourished in southeastern Turkey approximately 11,500 years ago, during the Pre-Pottery Neolithic period. The term encompasses a network of early ritual centers and settlements that were scattered across the Şanlıurfa region, with Göbekli Tepe and Karahan Tepe standing out as the most prominent and well-studied sites. These archaeological wonders have fundamentally altered our understanding of early human civilization and religious practices. The Tas Tepeler sites predate the advent of agriculture and settled societies, challenging long-held beliefs about the development of complex human organizations and spiritual expression.

Göbekli Tepe, discovered in 1994 by German archaeologist Klaus Schmidt, serves as the most famous example of Tas Tepeler culture. This site features a series of circular structures, each containing massive T-shaped stone pillars, some reaching heights of 5.5 meters. These pillars, intricately carved with animal reliefs and abstract symbols, hint at a sophisticated symbolic language and artistic tradition that existed millennia before the invention of writing.

Karahan Tepe, located about 35 kilometers east of Göbekli Tepe, represents another significant Tas Tepeler site. Discovered in 1997, it shares many architectural similarities with its more famous counterpart, including the presence of T-shaped pillars and circular structures. The proximity and similarity of these sites suggest a shared cultural tradition spanning a considerable area. What makes the Tas Tepeler culture particularly remarkable is the level of social organization and architectural skill it demonstrates. The construction of these monumental structures would have required the coordinated effort of many individuals over extended periods. This implies a degree of social complexity previously thought impossible for hunter-gatherer societies.

The purpose of these sites remains a subject of ongoing debate among archaeologists. Although they are generally believed to have served ritual or ceremonial functions, the exact nature of the practices conducted at them remains shrouded in mystery. The abundance of animal imagery in the stone carvings suggests a strong connection to the natural world, possibly reflecting the hunter-gatherer lifestyle of the builders. In his work on Karahan Tepe, Andrew Collins (2024) suggests these beings were likely a memory of the prime movers behind the Tas Tepeler culture—ancient shamans who had mastered the art of communion with the cosmic and otherworldly through altered states of consciousness.

As I reflected further, it became clear that the Anunnaki were not just external deities arriving from the sky; they were, in many ways, intermediaries between the physical and astral realms. The Apkallu, often depicted in Mesopotamian texts as semi-divine sages, could be understood as the otherworldly entities that the Anunnaki, or more precisely, shamans, made contact with during their vision quests. These encounters with the Apkallu through astral journeys allowed these early shamanic figures to access hidden realms of knowledge, much like those who report communing with entities during modern DMT experiences.

Through these astral connections, the Anunnaki learned the arts and sciences that would eventually become the foundation of civilization. They gained knowledge of agriculture, architecture, and other advancements, not through trial and error but by accessing higher dimensions where such wisdom was readily available. This knowledge, once acquired, was then brought back to the earthly realm and shared with other communities—like the Ubaid people—where the Anunnaki were seen as divine beings, gods who had descended from the stars. It's much like the phenomenon of cargo cults, where technologically advanced visitors are deified by those less familiar with their innovations.

Thus, the Anunnaki could be considered divine leaders who determined the fates of humans. These fates, or *mes* are the incantations and divine teachings etched on the Tablet of Destinies, much like the *Key of Solomon*, a powerful grimoire that provides detailed instructions for summoning and controlling spiritual entities through rituals, symbols, and incantations. For occultists and secret societies, this text holds immense significance as it represents the pursuit of hidden knowledge and mastery over the unseen forces that govern the universe. Much like the Tablet of Destinies, which bestows control over fate, the *Key of Solomon* is a spiritual tool that enables its possessor to command both celestial and infernal beings, thereby gaining influence over the material and spiritual worlds. Both are believed to function as conduits for transcendent knowledge, offering the means to shape reality and the course of human destiny.

The keepers of this knowledge, the Anunnaki, were revered because of their ability to bridge the gap between worlds. However, not all of humanity was granted access to this sacred knowledge. As the Sumerian myths tell us, only a select few were allowed to partake in the mysteries of the universe until Enki, one of the Anunnaki, rebelled against the established order. Much like the serpent in the biblical tale of Eden, Enki broke ranks and gave humanity the gift of discernment—the knowledge of good and evil, and more importantly, the path to mastery over the mystical arts. Enki is also depicted with serpent symbolism and motif.

In this act of rebellion, humanity "became like the gods," learning the sacred mysteries that had previously been hidden from them. This was not merely about ethical discernment but about gaining access to the astral plane, where the true quest—the search for the tree of life—began. The Apkallu, or these otherworldly entities, hold the key to immortality, the real goal being to stop rival forces from mastering the astral plane and gaining control of the most sacred technology: *immortality*.

This is the deeper truth behind the Anunnaki saga. It's not simply a story of godlike beings who descended from the heavens to rule over humans; it's a tale of ancient shamans who mastered the art of astral travel, communed with powerful entities, and sought the most sacred knowledge that could grant them immortality. The kings and lugals of the ancient world, particularly those of noble blood, retained the innate ability to commune with these entities because the astral light, as occultists like Eliphas Levi have taught, resides in the blood. This notion of bloodlines and their connection to astral power became the foundation for many of the royal and priestly traditions that followed.

The rituals and magic passed down through these bloodlines were not for the masses, but eventually, the masses would have their eyes opened, much like the large gazing eyes of the Sumerian votives. This could be through contact with the nomadic shamans who shared their knowledge of sacred plants and how to access altered states of consciousness, or in some cases, there may not have been contact with an Anunnaki intermediary at all. Since the astral realm is accessible to all, any human who stumbles upon the sacred mushroom or flower can lift the veil and begin communion with the entities. This is the real meaning of the eucharist; *communio*, a mystical participation in the divine, not just through ritualistic consumption but through the transformative act of directly accessing hidden realms. The wide eyes of the Sumerian votives may symbolize this opening of consciousness, a gaze into the unseen world, where communion is not merely symbolic but a direct experience of the divine. In this sense, the act of communion is the ultimate unlocking of sacred knowledge, where the veil is lifted, and one begins to truly "see" the deeper reality that lies beyond the physical.

This communion was reserved for a select few who were considered worthy of mastering the astral plane. In this sense, the Anunnaki weren't just gods or rulers, they were gatekeepers of the most profound and secretive knowledge, guarding the path to immortality, the ultimate power, and the mysteries of the cosmos. As I studied the myths, the archaeological record, and the altered-state experiences reported across cultures, a pattern began to emerge. It suggested that what we call the Anunnaki in the ancient texts might reflect two interconnected layers of reality rather than a single kind of being. The first layer may have been the Anunnaki themselves, not gods in the literal sense but human elites or shamanic survivors of the Younger Dryas upheavals. They could have carried advanced knowledge of agriculture, astronomy, and consciousness-altering practices, becoming the custodians of civilization in the eyes of those who followed them. The second layer is what the Sumerians called the Apkallu, discarnate intelligences or otherworldly presences that shamans across cultures have described for millennia. These beings exist outside ordinary perception yet can be contacted in expanded states of consciousness, sometimes aided by entheogens such as the opium poppy. From this perspective, the Anunnaki would have been human intermediaries bridging the physical world and the realm of the Apkallu. Ancient accounts of "knowledge descending from the heavens" could then be understood as the transmission of wisdom accessed through altered states, where human shamans communed with ultraterrestrial intelligences rather than meeting physical visitors from the sky.

To commune with them was to access realms far beyond mortal comprehension, where the boundaries of life and death dissolved, and one could transcend the limits of human existence. This was the sacred path, one few dared to walk, and those who succeeded became the keepers of knowledge passed down through bloodlines, ensuring the legacy of the Anunnaki endured. With the veil lifted, ancient secrets spilled forth, igniting a silent war for control of humanity's forgotten past. The true battle for control over these mysteries would soon unfold.

CHAPTER 6

THE REVELATION
Cosmic Vessels and Interdimensional Beings

We are not human beings having a spiritual experience. We are spiritual beings having a human experience.

—PIERRE TEILHARD DE CHARDIN

As a long-time seeker, I have been drawn to various mystery schools, research groups, and occult societies. (Consider that a confession.) I have studied magic and the occult for twenty years. In fact, I once rode my bike to an occult bookstore when I was eight and sneaked inside the eighteen-and-older section, where I first read *Buckland's Complete Book of Witchcraft* and Aleister Crowley's *The Book of the Law.* So if you count that, over thirty years.

It was during a recent occult study that I thought I might revisit those days as a child in the church pew, hoping to hear the voice of God. After weeks of experimenting with various meditation techniques I had been given by the esoteric group I was corresponding with, I began to sense an unsettling presence during my sessions. It wasn't exactly malevolent, but it didn't feel benign either. Worried, and seeking guidance, I reached out to Opus Sanctorum Angelorum, or the Work of the Holy Angels. This is a Catholic movement dedicated to spreading devotion to and cooperation with the holy angels. Founded in 1949, it has a complex history with the Vatican, having undergone scrutiny and reforms in the 1990s to align more closely with official Church teachings. Today, it operates under the supervision of the Vatican, specifically the Congregation for the Doctrine of the Faith.

I was put in touch with a priest there who we will call Father John, a priest associated with Opus Sanctorum Angelorum. After explaining my situation, he listened patiently before speaking.

"What you're experiencing is not uncommon for those who dabble in occult practices," Father John said, his voice calm but concerned. "But before we address that, I want to introduce you to a powerful spiritual concept from one of the great Doctors of the Church, St. Teresa of Avila's Interior Castle."

"Teresa's work," Father John continued, "offers profound insights into spiritual growth and the discernment of spirits. It's particularly relevant to your situation."

He went on to explain that the Interior Castle, also known as The Mansions, is a spiritual guidebook written by the sixteenth-century Spanish mystic and Carmelite nun, St. Teresa of Avila. In this work, she describes the soul as a crystal castle containing seven mansions, representing the journey of faith through prayer and meditation.

The mansion, Father John elaborated, describes the soul's progression from the outer regions of prayer and self-knowledge to the innermost chambers where union with God occurs. Along this journey, Teresa warns, a person will encounter various spiritual dangers and deceptions, including those that might come from malevolent spiritual entities.

He paused, allowing me to absorb this information before continuing. "What's crucial here is that St. Teresa's approach is rooted in Christian tradition and approved by the Church. It's a safe and profound way to deepen your spiritual life, unlike the occult practices you've been experimenting with."

Father John then introduced the concept of discernment. "Discernment," he explained, "is the ability to distinguish between spirits, to recognize what comes from God and what does not. It's a skill that Teresa herself had to develop, and one that's crucial for anyone engaging in deep spiritual practices."

He went on to emphasize the importance of discernment in navigating spiritual experiences. "Developing the gift of discernment is crucial. Not every spiritual encounter is beneficial, even if it seems harmless or even positive at first. The devil can disguise himself as an angel of light."

St. Teresa of Avila, I learned, was a revered mystic and Doctor of the Catholic Church who described an encounter with a being of light in her autobiography that has intrigued scholars and theologians for centuries. This being, which she perceived in "bodily form" and described as "not tall but short, and very beautiful," appeared to her with a golden spear that it plunged into her heart, causing a mix of intense pain and profound spiritual ecstasy (Pasulka, 2020). While Teresa interpreted this experience within the framework of Catholic theology, noting the being as an angel, her description deviates from traditional theological accounts, leading to questions about the true nature of her vision. The tension between her account and established angelology suggests that Teresa's encounter might not fit neatly into the religious context she knew, potentially opening the door to alternative interpretations (Pasulka, 2020). Given the being's physical presence and the light it emitted, could Teresa's vision could be reinterpreted as an encounter with an extraterrestrial entity or even an Apkallu?

Santa Teresa de Jesús *by Francisco de Zurbarán. This painting, created by the renowned Spanish Baroque painter Francisco de Zurbarán, depicts Santa Teresa de Jesús (Saint Teresa of Ávila), a prominent Spanish mystic, writer, and reformer of the Carmelite Order.*

As I sat quietly, reflecting on the daunting implications of the research I'd uncovered, the weight of history seemed to press down on me. The allure of cosmic power—the kind that could sway the fate of civilizations—is not merely a distant myth or the musings of fringe theorists. It's a tangible thread that has woven its way through the fabric of human history, from the divine right of kings to the clandestine pursuits of modern secret societies. This thread has entangled not only the powerful and ambitious but also the curious and the desperate—those who, like me, have spent years searching for the truth behind the legends.

The idea that reality might be layered with hidden dimensions accessible only to a chosen few is as old as civilization itself. This notion is both thrilling and terrifying. What if those ancient stories of the Anunnaki—gods walking among humans—were not mere allegories but remnants of a forgotten truth? A truth both guarded and sought by those who believe that unlocking it could lead to ultimate power, or even immortality.

I couldn't help but wonder: Is it possible that our reality is just one layer of a much larger, more complex existence? An existence where the boundaries between the physical and the metaphysical blur, where entities like the Anunnaki still exert their influence in ways we are only beginning to understand? This question has haunted me for years, driving me deeper into the study of ancient texts, secretive societies, and modern technological advancements. What I've found suggests that the search for the power of the Anunnaki and the quest for the Tablet of Destinies is not just a relic of the past but a continuing saga, evolving with time, adapting to new contexts and new players.

While navigating the world of occult societies and mysterious bloodlines that claim descent from otherworldly beings, I found myself increasingly drawn to the intersections between ancient myths and modern science. The end of the previous chapter left us at the threshold of understanding how ancient myths can be weaponized in the pursuit of power, and how the concept of the Tablet of Destinies has influenced not just the ancient world but modern ideologies as well. Now, we turn our attention to the present, where these same ancient concepts are being reinterpreted through the lens of contemporary science and technology.

The search for truth about human origins and consciousness has led me down many unexpected paths in my career as an archaeologist and historian. What I'm about to reveal challenges the very foundations of how we understand ourselves and our place in the cosmos. The evidence points to a startling conclusion: Humans are essentially vessels—containers for consciousness that originates beyond our physical forms. This revelation isn't entirely new. Ancient cultures and esoteric traditions have hinted at this reality for millennia. The Gnostics spoke of *archons*—cosmic jailers who trapped divine sparks in human bodies. Vedic scriptures describe *maya*, the illusory nature of material existence. But it's only now, with advances in quantum physics and consciousness research, that we can begin to scientifically grapple with these age-old concepts.

Central to this perennial wisdom is the idea of non-duality, which teaches that all of reality is interconnected and unified. This awareness, called *gnosis* in the West and *jnana* in the East, is about realizing that our individual self is deeply connected to a greater, divine reality. The path to this non-dual realization involves the purification of the mind and heart, the cultivation of virtues, and the practice of contemplative disciplines. This wisdom forms the thread that connects ancient myths to modern accounts of extraterrestrial encounters, from reports of demonic possession to psychedelic visions of self-replicating machine elves.

To grasp the magnitude of this revelation, we must shed the constraints of purely materialist thinking and embrace a more holistic view of reality. Swiss psychiatrist Carl Gustav Jung posited the existence of a collective unconscious, a shared reservoir of experiences and symbols that transcends individual minds and cultures. Jung's concept of archetypes provides a crucial foundation for understanding the persistent appearance of similar entities across diverse cultures and epochs. These archetypes are universal, archaic patterns and images that derive from the collective unconscious and are the psychic counterpart of instinct. This realm, existing outside ordinary time and space, is the source of primordial patterns and images that shape both the inner and outer dimensions of reality. The language of myth—neither rational nor irrational, but pre-rational—expresses these truths through symbols and archetypes, personified as gods, heroes, and other numinous figures.

When we synthesize these various strands of thought—Jungian archetypes, phenomenology, quantum consciousness, and higher-dimensional physics—a new paradigm begins to emerge. This paradigm suggests that what we perceive as reality is but a thin slice of a much vaster, multidimensional existence. The entities that have populated our myths, religions, and modern encounters may be manifestations of archetypal forces that exist in these higher dimensions, interacting with our consciousness in ways that we are only beginning to understand.

The Gnostic traditions offer another perspective on these entities; they speak of *archons*—powerful beings that ruled over the material world and influenced human affairs. According to Gnostic belief, these archons were created by a flawed being called the *Demiurge*, a creator god, and stood as obstacles between humanity and the true, transcendent benevolent God. This cosmology suggests a more complex view of these entities, portraying them as both impediments to spiritual enlightenment and potential guides (Filoramo, 1990).

The archons, far from being mere symbolic representations of oppressive forces, are believed to be literal cosmic entities wielding vast power over both the physical realm and the human psyche. This hierarchical structure of cosmic rulers bears a striking resemblance to the pantheon of Anunnaki deities in Mesopotamian mythology, with its complex relationships and spheres of influence. The connection between the archons and the Anunnaki is not merely coincidental but deeply symbolic, reflecting an ancient understanding of time and space as domains governed by powerful, often unseen forces (Apocryphon of John, second century).

The Gnostic portrayal of the archons as cosmic deceivers, dedicated to keeping humanity ignorant of its true divine nature, provides a stark contrast to the more benevolent depictions of deities in other religious traditions. These entities are not here to guide or protect humanity but to maintain a state of ignorance and subjugation, creating a false reality that humans accept as the only reality. Gnostic and Jungian views converge in their recognition of powerful, often unseen forces that shape human experience. These forces, whether conceived as archons or archetypes, are not simply external entities but are deeply embedded in the human psyche. They represent the darker aspects of our nature—the parts of ourselves that we often try to deny or repress. Understanding these forces can provide profound insights into both our individual and collective psyche, offering a path toward greater self-awareness and spiritual growth (Jung, 1960).

The exploration of ancient mythologies often reveals overlapping narratives that offer deeper insights into the beliefs and worldviews of early civilizations. The Abyss (similar to Abzu) and the Anunnaki have intrigued scholars and researchers for centuries, not only for their central roles in ancient Sumerian and Babylonian cultures but also for their intersections with interpretations of Yahweh, the deity central to the Abrahamic faiths. These mythological elements, often translated as deep bodies of water, may represent more complex concepts as described in ancient texts and depicted on artifacts like cylinder seals (Black and Green, 1992).

In biblical texts, the Abyss is often mentioned as a hidden door or gateway located near the Euphrates River, possibly beneath the ruins of the ancient city of Eridu. This concept is strikingly similar to the Sumerian "Abzu," associated with the god Enki, who is depicted as the creator of humanity (Bottéro, 1992). Enki's role as the Lord of the Abzu, where he built the temple E.ABZU, suggests that the Abyss may not be a physical body of water but rather a spiritual or dimensional gateway—something accessed and controlled in a non-literal sense. This theme of creation, manipulation, and control is central to understanding the true nature of the Anunnaki and their possible connection to the Apkallu, the bringers of civilization and knowledge to humanity.

The Apkallu, emerging from the primordial waters of the Abzu, are credited with bestowing upon early societies the essential arts of writing, agriculture, and city-building (van Buren, 1950). Their role as bearers of divine wisdom offers a compelling parallel to the Kabbalistic concept of Chokmah, the *sefirah* representing the first point of conscious intellect within creation (Scholem, 1946). In exploring these ancient mythologies and the concept of the abyss, we encounter not just physical and metaphysical voids but also psychological and existential depths—a perilous journey, as Friedrich Nietzsche warned: "He who fights with monsters should be careful lest he thereby become a monster. And if you gaze long enough into an abyss, the abyss will gaze back into you" (Nietzsche, 1989).

The understanding of Yahweh, originally one among many deities, evolved over millennia. In Gnostic cosmology, Yahweh takes on a more sinister role, identified with the Demiurge. This depiction of Yahweh as a deluded being, unaware of the higher spiritual realities above him, parallels the portrayal of the Anunnaki as beings who exert control over humanity, often through deception and manipulation (Filoramo, 1990).

The question of whether Yahweh could be an Anunnaki is provocative. Some interpretations suggest that Yahweh may have been an extraterrestrial being, a member of the Anunnaki who played a significant role in shaping human history. This view, supported by parallels between Yahweh's actions in the Old Testament and the behavior of the Anunnaki as described in Sumerian myths, adds another layer of complexity to our understanding of these ancient entities (Sitchin, 1976).

The figure of Sabaoth, the rebel archon in Gnostic mythology, embodies a recurring motif of divine rebellion that echoes across various mythological traditions. By examining Sabaoth in relation to similar figures such as Enki, Lucifer, and Prometheus, we can discern a fundamental archetype reflecting deep-seated aspects of human consciousness and spiritual aspiration. These narratives of divine rebellion speak to the human impulse to question authority, seek higher knowledge, and transcend perceived limitations (Campbell, 1949).

In the modern era, these archetypal entities have taken on new forms that reflect our evolving understanding of the cosmos. The nineteenth and early twentieth centuries saw a surge of interest in spiritualism and theosophy, which claimed contact with ascended masters and spiritual guides from other planes of existence. These movements represented a continuation of humanity's age-old quest to communicate with entities beyond the veil of ordinary reality (Hanegraaff, 1996).

The twentieth century witnessed a dramatic shift in the manifestation of these entities with the rise of UFO phenomena and accounts of extraterrestrial encounters. The archetypal wise beings from the stars found new expression in reports of alien visitations and abductions. The image of the "grey alien" became a dominant motif in popular culture and personal accounts, echoing the work of Bob Lazar, who claimed to have worked on reverse-engineering extraterrestrial technology at Area 51 (Lazar, 1989). Lazar's stories align with ancient narratives of seeking hidden knowledge—knowledge that, if harnessed, could alter the very fabric of our reality.

The parallels between Lazar's claims and the ancient search for the Tablet of Destinies are striking. Both involve the pursuit of objects or knowledge that could grant supreme power, transcending the ordinary limitations of humanity. Lazar's tale of bending space-time harks back to the legends of the Anunnaki, who were said to possess the ability to manipulate the very forces of the universe. But Lazar's story is just one thread in a much larger tapestry of modern-day quests for ultimate power.

The US government's exploration of the Gateway Process—a technique developed in the 1970s to expand human consciousness—reveals how ancient esoteric practices have been repurposed in the context of modern science. The Gateway Process, which involves the use of binaural beats, hypnosis, and meditation to access altered states of consciousness, is strikingly similar to the rituals of the Magi, who sought to commune with otherworldly entities through the consumption of Haoma and other intoxicants (CIA, 2003). Just as the Magi believed their rituals could grant them access to divine knowledge, the Gateway Process was designed to enable participants to transcend the physical world and explore non-ordinary states of consciousness.

In 538 BCE, when Cyrus the Great of Persia conquered Babylon, a profound cultural and religious transformation began that would reverberate through millennia. The Persians, adherents of

Zoroastrianism, a religion influenced by the Kabbalistic cult of the dying-god, gave rise to the cult of the Magi. Their secretive practices involved the use of Haoma, a sacred and intoxicating plant believed to grant immortality, echoing the biblical Tree of Knowledge (Plutarch, 1927; Zaehner, 1961). This theme of forbidden knowledge, central to the story of Adam and Eve, would later be mirrored in the philosophies of Gnosticism and Hermeticism, both of which sought to transcend the material world through esoteric knowledge (Filoramo, 1990).

The liberation of the Jewish people by Cyrus allowed these mystical traditions to spread across the ancient world, influencing Greek philosophy. Figures like Pythagoras and Plato integrated these doctrines into their teachings, laying the groundwork for the development of the Hellenistic mystery religions, including Orphism and the Dionysian Mysteries, which involved the use of psychoactive substances to achieve states of divine possession (Pliny, 1855).

These ancient traditions laid the foundation for the transhumanist movement of the modern era. Transhumanism, while presenting itself as a scientific endeavor, is deeply rooted in the esoteric philosophies that have driven humanity's quest for transcendence for millennia. The movement's goal of achieving a post-human existence through technology mirrors the Gnostic aspiration to escape the limitations of the material world and unite with the divine (Bostrom, 2005).

A key figure in the transhumanist movement is Ray Kurzweil, who advanced artificial intelligence and longevity research. Kurzweil's concept of the *singularity*, a moment when AI surpasses human intelligence and merges with human consciousness, is reminiscent of the ancient belief in becoming as gods through knowledge (Kurzweil, 2005). This idea, central to both Gnosticism and Hermeticism, has been repurposed in the digital age as the ultimate goal of transhumanism.

The connections between ancient esotericism and modern technology are evident in the work of Bob Lazar and the Gateway Process. Lazar's claims about reverse-engineering extraterrestrial technology align with the alchemical quest to manipulate the fundamental forces of nature—a pursuit linked to the occult (Lazar, 1989). Similarly, the Gateway Process reflects the enduring interest in unlocking the mysteries of the mind and exploring realms beyond our ordinary perception.

The influence of esoteric traditions on modern psychology is also significant. Carl Jung's concept of the collective unconscious, a repository of shared human experiences and archetypes, mirrors the Gnostic belief in a universal mind or Nous (Jung, 1960). Jung's interest in alchemy, seen as a symbolic process of psychological transformation, further illustrates the connection between ancient esoteric traditions and modern psychology. The convergence of ancient esotericism and modern technology is also evident in the field of cybernetics, which has played a key role in the development of artificial intelligence. A cybernetic vision of a world where machines and humans are seamlessly integrated reflects the transhumanist aspiration to transcend the limitations of the physical body and achieve a state of godhood. This vision, while presented as a scientific and rational endeavor, is deeply rooted in the esoteric traditions that have driven humanity's quest for transcendence for millennia (Wiener, 1948). This idea, popularized by Ray Kurzweil, is reminiscent of the apocalyptic visions of the end times found in various religious traditions. The singularity is seen as a moment of transformation, where humanity transcends its physical limitations and merges with the divine (Kurzweil, 2005).

Concurrently with the rise of UFO phenomena, explorers of altered states of consciousness reported encounters with beings that seemed to exist in realms beyond ordinary reality.

Ethnobotanist Terence McKenna, in his explorations with psychedelic substances, described encounters with "machine elves" or "self-transforming machine elves," entities that appear to inhabit a realm beyond our conventional three-dimensional reality (McKenna, 1992). In addition to ethnobotany, Terence McKenna was intrigued by philosophy. He proposed that psychedelic plants, particularly psilocybin-containing mushrooms, played a crucial role in human cognitive evolution. He argued that the consumption of these substances by early hominids could have accelerated the development of language, abstract thinking, and cultural complexity (McKenna, 1992, 24–30). While McKenna's stoned ape theory remains controversial in academic circles, it offers an intriguing framework for understanding the potential evolutionary significance of psychedelic experiences.

The similarities between these various manifestations—their role as intermediaries, their association with knowledge and transformation, and their ability to interact with human consciousness—suggest a common origin or essence. This brings us to the crux of our revelation: These entities, in all their diverse forms, are manifestations of the same archetypal forces that the ancient Sumerians knew as the Anunnaki. The Anunnaki, far from being merely anthropomorphic deities of ancient Mesopotamia, represent a fundamental aspect of reality that exists outside the constraints of our physical universe. They are, in essence, archetypal forces that manifest through human consciousness and imagination. This understanding aligns with Gnostic and Kabbalistic models of reality, positing the existence of higher realms populated by spiritual entities that influence the material world (Scholem, 1946).

To better grasp this concept, we must consider the etymology and meaning of words such as *persona*, *personality*, and *personification*. These terms all derive from the Latin *persona*, meaning "mask." This linguistic connection reveals a profound truth: The various forms these entities take are essentially masks or avatars through which they interact with our reality.

The anthropologist Joseph Campbell's concept of "The Hero with a Thousand Faces" provides further insight into this phenomenon. Campbell demonstrated how mythological heroes across cultures share common traits and story arcs, suggesting an underlying archetypal structure (Campbell, 1949). In the same way, the Anunnaki—as archetypal forces—adopt different "masks" or manifestations across cultures and time periods while retaining their essential nature.

This process of manifestation occurs through what occultists and some psychologists refer to as *egregores* or *thoughtforms*—collective mental constructs that can take on a life of their own. The human mind, through its creative and imaginative faculties, serves as a conduit for these archetypal forces to take shape and interact with our reality. This shared creative process shows how these beings can appear in new forms in different cultures over time (Durkheim, 2001; Jung, 1960).

The concept of egregores finds parallels in modern psychological and sociological theories. The French sociologist Émile Durkheim's notion of *collective representations*—shared mental concepts that form the basis of social cohesion—bears a resemblance to the idea of egregores (Durkheim, 2001). Similarly, Carl Jung's concept of the collective unconscious can be seen as a scientific approach to understanding the same phenomena that occultists describe as egregores.

From this perspective, the Anunnaki can be understood as primordial archetypes that have been clothed in various cultural and historical garments throughout human history. The gods of ancient Sumer, the angels and demons of Abrahamic traditions, the extraterrestrial visitors of modern UFO lore—all can be seen as manifestations of these underlying archetypal forces.

This understanding challenges our conventional notions of time and causality. If the Anunnaki exist as eternal archetypes beyond space and time, then their influence on human consciousness is not limited to a linear historical progression. Instead, we might conceive of a kind of temporal resonance, where these archetypal forces echo across time, influencing human culture and consciousness in complex, nonlinear ways.

The implications of this revelation are profound. It suggests that the myths, religions, and spiritual traditions of humanity are not mere cultural constructs or primitive attempts to explain natural phenomena but rather glimpses of a deeper reality that transcends our ordinary perception. The wisdom encoded in these traditions may, in fact, represent a kind of user's manual for interacting with these higher-dimensional forces.

Furthermore, this understanding provides a framework for reconciling seemingly contradictory accounts of entity encounters across cultures and time periods. The apparent differences between, say, an angelic visitation described by a medieval mystic and a modern alien abduction experience can be understood as different cultural translations of encounters with the same underlying archetypal forces.

This new understanding also sheds light on the persistent human fascination with the idea of "ancient aliens" or advanced civilizations intervening in human history. While the literal interpretation of such ideas may be questionable from a historical and archaeological standpoint, they can be understood as modern mythological expressions of humanity's ongoing interaction with these archetypal forces (Sitchin, 1976).

The question then arises: How can we, as embodied beings in a physical reality, access or interact with these discarnate entities? The answer lies in altered states of consciousness, which have been utilized by shamans, mystics, and seekers throughout history to pierce the veil between worlds. These altered states represent a shift in perception and cognition that allows individuals to experience reality beyond the confines of ordinary waking consciousness (Strassman, 2001).

Ancient Mesopotamian priests and magi were adept at entering these altered states, often through ritualistic practices, to commune with the Anunnaki and gain wisdom and power (Zaehner, 1961). These practices typically involved a combination of physical, mental, and spiritual techniques designed to shift consciousness and open channels of communication with the divine. One of the most common methods employed by ancient cultures to achieve altered states was the use of entheogens. These substances were believed to facilitate direct communication with the gods and access to divine wisdom (Ruck et al., 1979). In modern times, various methods have been employed to achieve similar states of consciousness. The use of entheogens, particularly DMT, has been reported to facilitate encounters with entities that bear striking resemblances to the archetypal beings described in ancient traditions (Strassman, 2001).

Rick Strassman's groundbreaking research with DMT in the 1990s provided some of the first scientifically documented accounts of entity encounters in altered states. Many of Strassman's subjects reported meetings with beings they described as aliens, angels, or elves, often in settings that seemed to exist outside of conventional reality (Strassman, 2001). These modern experiences bear striking similarities to traditional shamanic journeys and mystical visions. The entities encountered often impart knowledge, perform healing, or provide guidance, much like the gods and spirits of ancient myths. This consistency across cultures and time periods suggests that these experiences may be tapping into a common source—the realm of archetypal entities we have identified as the Anunnaki. Are these experiences with entities encountered while in altered state merely hallucinations produced by an altered brain state, or do they represent genuine contacts with independently existing intelligences? The answer may lie somewhere between these extremes, in a perspective that recognizes the co-creative nature of consciousness and reality.

The Gateway Process, developed by Robert Monroe and adopted by the CIA, offers a fascinating glimpse into the potential of human consciousness. This classified project aimed to alter consciousness, allowing participants to access intuitive knowledge and other dimensions (CIA, 2003). Declassified documents reveal that during these experiments, participants frequently encountered interdimensional entities, often described as reptilian humanoids. These experiences bear a striking resemblance to accounts from various spiritual and shamanic traditions, as well as modern UFO encounters. The consistency of these reports across cultures and time periods suggests we may be dealing with a fundamental aspect of reality long obscured by our limited perceptions.

The use of entheogens—substances that generate the divine within—has been integral to human spiritual practices for millennia. From the soma of ancient India to the kykeon of the Eleusinian Mysteries, these substances have been revered for their ability to open doors of perception and facilitate direct experiences of the divine. Modern research into psychedelics is now rediscovering their potential for healing trauma, treating depression, and catalyzing profound spiritual experiences (Griffiths et al., 2006). However, it's crucial to approach these realms with caution and discernment. The entities encountered in altered states of consciousness, whether induced by meditation, breathwork, or psychedelics, are not necessarily benevolent. Just as in the physical world, the realms beyond our ordinary perception may contain both helpful and harmful influences. The challenge lies in developing the wisdom to navigate these experiences safely and integrate their insights into our lives.

The concept of humans as "containers of souls" or vessels for consciousness finds echoes in various spiritual and philosophical traditions. In the Joe Rogan podcast, Jeremy Corbell and George Knapp discussed the possibility that humans were genetically engineered by nonhuman intelligence for nefarious purposes (Rogan, 2024). This idea aligns with Bob Lazar's claim that extraterrestrials viewed humans as "containers of souls" (Lazar, 1989). If we were to accept that human consciousness can interact with archetypal forces that shape reality, it opens up new possibilities for human growth and development. Techniques for accessing altered states of consciousness and communicating with these entities could be refined and applied in fields ranging from psychology to creativity and innovation. But if our thoughts and intentions can influence the manifestation of reality, what responsibility do we bear for the world we create?

The great challenge of our time is to articulate this perennial wisdom in a way that is relevant and meaningful for the modern world. We live in an age of unprecedented change and complexity, a time of ecological crisis, social upheaval, and spiritual yearning. The old myths and paradigms are crumbling, and a new story is struggling to be born. This new story affirms that we are not alone in this universe, but rather part of a vast and interconnected whole, a cosmic community that includes all beings, visible and invisible.

Transhumanism and the AI revolution are just stops along the quest for immortality. This esoteric alchemical practice reflects humanity's enduring desire to transcend the limitations of the physical body and achieve a higher state of existence. This quest, deeply rooted in ancient traditions and spanning cultures, continues to influence modern practices and beliefs, like transhumanism, artificial intelligence, and the pursuit of the singularity. From the origin of our species to the dawn of consciousness, we now stand on the cusp of a great transformation. This transformation isn't about attaining godlike power over others or the natural world. It's about realizing our inherent divine nature and acting from a place of profound wisdom and compassion. The revelation of our nature as vessels of consciousness challenges us to expand our understanding of reality and our place within it. It invites us to explore the vast potentials lying dormant within us, while also recognizing our profound interconnectedness with all of existence.

As we push through this brave new world, we will have to consider whether AI can truly achieve consciousness or merely simulate it convincingly. This, we should also question of our own evolution. Nietzsche asked if, after the "death of God," we must "become gods ourselves simply to appear worthy of it." If we attain such status, might we still be imposters? Will we become gods or only "appear" to be so? Are we truly tapping into some cosmic potential, or are we simply very convincing simulacra of what we imagine greatness to be? Perhaps in creating AI, we're confronting a mirror of our own nature—entities striving to simulate a consciousness they may never truly possess, much like the Anunnaki themselves.

EPILOGUE

Humanity's Cosmic Destiny: Embracing Our Hidden Potential

As we've explored the connections and revelations of the Anunnaki, we find ourselves facing a profound paradox. The very truths that could illuminate our path forward often lie shrouded in the mists of esoteric tradition, accessible only to those who have undertaken the arduous journey of self-discovery. This is not mere gatekeeping, but a recognition of a fundamental principle: that unearned wisdom is not only unappreciated but potentially dangerous. Terence McKenna (1992) alluded to this in his warning about experimenting with psychedelics.

Consider the paradoxical duty of the occult adept. Having wandered the labyrinthine paths of arcane knowledge, the adept finds themselves in possession of profound truths. Yet these truths demand not to be freely dispensed, but to be carefully guarded and judiciously revealed. This principle echoes through the structure of the "hero's journey," a pattern so deeply ingrained in our collective psyche that it forms the foundation of countless myths across cultures. The hero, called to adventure, encounters a mentor who possesses the knowledge the hero seeks. However, the mentor does not simply hand over the treasured wisdom.

Instead, they provide guidance, perhaps a tool or talisman, but ultimately they send the hero forth to face trials alone.

Why this seeming cruelty? Why not spare the hero the ordeal and simply impart the needed knowledge? The answer lies in the nature of true wisdom. It is not a commodity to be transferred, but a state of being to be achieved. The mentor understands that interfering too directly would rob the hero of the experiences necessary for growth and transformation.

As the hero progresses, they face ordeals, enter the belly of the beast, pass through the flames, and eventually emerge transformed, often with an elixir—the gift of the goddess, to use Campbell's terminology (Campbell, 1949). Does the hero emerge a phoenix from the ashes? Here, at the moment of triumph, lies a critical choice that will determine whether the hero's journey serves a greater purpose or becomes a cautionary tale.

If the hero chooses to keep the treasure for themselves, retreating into a hedonic tower, they risk becoming that which they once fought against. Like Smaug atop his pile of gold, they become the very dragon that future heroes must face in the ordeal. The dragon, hoarding the treasure, is so bloated with the flame that the very act of exhalation threatens to destroy the hero who has come to challenge its dominion. The flame embodies the dual nature of existence itself—both life-giving and destructive. In understanding this duality, we can turn to the Hegelian principle of thesis and antithesis. Hegel's dialectic suggests that every idea or force (thesis) naturally encounters its opposite (antithesis). These opposites are not merely conflicting forces; they are essential to the process of growth and evolution. The true resolution comes in the synthesis, where these opposites are reconciled into a higher unity, leading to transformation.

In this light, the flame is not simply a force of destruction or creation; it is the synthesis of both. It is a transformative power that renews and purifies by bringing together opposites. This dialectical process mirrors the natural cycles of life and death, birth and rebirth, where the tension between opposing forces generates new forms of existence. The journey, then, is not merely about achieving personal enlightenment, but about what one does with that enlightenment. How does this understanding manifest in our modern conception of human growth and potential?

Abraham Maslow, a pioneering figure in modern psychology, recognized a similar truth in his later years (Maslow, 1968). His hierarchy of needs, often depicted as a pyramid, charts the path of human development from basic physiological needs to the pinnacle of self-actualization, a state of fulfilling one's potential. However, even Maslow came to understand that self-actualization, much like the hero's triumph, is not the final destination. This insight was profoundly influenced by his interactions with Viktor Frankl, a Holocaust survivor whose experiences led him to a deeper understanding of human motivation. Chronicled in his seminal work, *Man's Search for Meaning* (1946), Frankl's experiences in the concentration camps led him to a different conclusion about human motivation. While Maslow's hierarchy culminates in self-actualization, Frankl believed that this was not the ultimate goal. Instead, he introduced the concept of self-transcendence, the capacity to rise above oneself and find meaning through serving others. Frankl proposed that the highest human drive is not the pursuit of personal fulfillment (as in Maslow's model) but the search for meaning, even in the face of suffering.

In contrast to Nietzsche's assertion of a "will to power" (Nietzsche, 1989), Frankl argued for a "will to meaning." During his time in the concentration camps, Frankl observed that those who found a sense of purpose, even in the most dire circumstances, were more likely to survive. For example, he noticed that prisoners who focused on reuniting with loved ones or completing unfinished work they found meaningful were better able to endure the horrors of camp life. This led Frankl to conclude that meaning, rather than self-actualization or power, is the true driving force behind human behavior.

Frankl's insights prompted Maslow to reconsider his original pyramid. The missing capstone, Maslow realized, was self-transcendence, a recognition that the fulfillment of one's potential is not the final destination, but a step toward something greater. The missing capstone, then, is the act of sharing one's hard-won wisdom and guiding others on their journeys, a recognition that our fulfillment comes not from hoarding our achievements but from elevating others through them. Yet the path of returning to share the gift with one's community, is fraught with its own risks. Here, we must confront the harsh truth illustrated in Plato's allegory of the cave. The hero who has seen the light and returns to share it with those still bound in the shackles of the cave's darkness risks ridicule, rejection, and ultimately death. Those shackled in the cave are comfortable in the darkness, glimpsing only flickers of light and watching shadows dance across the cave walls. They love the stories they have created for their shadow puppets. They argue over the nature of the shadows, never venturing into the unknown outside the cave. Thus, they will lash out against any bearer of light. They fear being blinded by light but fail to understand it is the darkness that has taken their sight. The light is meant for those "with eyes to see."

The true hero's journey is not a straightforward ascent from ignorance to enlightenment, but a continuous cycle of growth. The hero who understands this knows that their role is not to drag others into the light, but to spark in them the desire to seek it themselves. As Plutarch wisely observed, people are not vessels to be filled, but flames to be kindled. You have a divine spark, wanting to shine brightly.

In this lies the true wisdom of re-*veiling*. To re-veil is not to obscure, but to present truth in a way that encourages exploration. It is to leave signs and symbols that guide others not to a fixed destination, but to the beginning of their own path. In this way, the hero evolves into the mentor, sowing seeds of curiosity that will blossom into new journeys. This cyclical nature of revelation and re-veiling reflects a truth about existence itself. In the Greek conception, a hero was not truly a hero without *kleos*—the glory that comes from having one's deeds sung and celebrated by others. This is not mere vanity, but a recognition of the interconnectedness of all journeys. We are all, simultaneously, heroes on our own quests and supporting characters in the quests of others.

When we embrace this perspective, we begin to see that in the course of our lives, we play not just one role, but many. We are the hero, setting forth on our journey of discovery. We are the mentor, guiding others with hard-won wisdom. We are the threshold guardian, testing others' readiness. We are the ally, offering aid in times of need. And yes, at times, we may even be the dragon, posing a necessary challenge for others to overcome. In fact, we are often the dragon to overcome in our own story, the final battle culminating in us not destroying the dragon, but integrating it into the grand unifying narrative of our redemption.

By consciously engaging with these various aspects of ourselves, we participate in a grand process of psychic integration. We become more whole, more fully human, by embracing the full spectrum of our potential. Yet this personal integration is but a microcosm of a grander, cosmic process. In Gnostic thought, we find the concept of *Pleroma*—the fullness of divine powers. Our journey of self-discovery and integration can be seen as a recapitulation of this cosmic wholeness. As above, so below; as within, so without. Each personal transformation ripples outward, contributing to the evolution of collective consciousness.

In this light, we can see each persona we adopt, each role we play, as a mask—one of the thousand faces of the hero described by Campbell. Yet these masks are not false faces worn to deceive, but aspects of our multifaceted true self, each revealing a different facet of the divine as it manifests through us.

Here we confront a profound realization: The veil spoken of in esoteric traditions, often thought to be an external barrier to divine understanding, is not separate from us at all. We are the creators and sustainers of this veil. Each of the thoughts, beliefs, and identities we cling to weaves into the intricate fabric that both hides and reveals the unity of all existence. The veil is a dynamic creation of our own consciousness, simultaneously obscuring and unveiling the deeper truths of the cosmos as we evolve. By engaging in the work of conscious evolution, we continuously lift and replace these veils, each revelation leading to new mysteries, each answered question spawning new inquiries. This is not a process with a final destination, but an eternal dance of discovery.

In this cosmic drama, we are simultaneously the actors and the audience, the playwright and the stage. Our task is not to conclude the cosmic play, but to enrich it, to live each moment with authenticity and depth. We are called to infuse the mundane with the sacred, to see the universal truths within the details of everyday life, and to recognize that the finite moments of our existence are reflections of the infinite. In this way, we contribute to the ongoing creation of the world, one conscious act at a time. The goal is *meaning*.

Our cosmic destiny is not something waiting for us in some distant future. It is here, now, unfolding in each choice we make, each role we play, each veil we lift and refashion. We are not separate from the universe, striving to find our place within it. We are the universe, becoming conscious of itself, playing out the greatest story ever told. As such, it is imperative that we accept that the path of the hero, the duty of the adept, and the journey of cosmic awakening are not separate endeavors, but facets of a single, grand undertaking. To navigate the complexities of our individual and collective evolution, we must do so with courage, wisdom, and a sense of wonder at the magnificent existence of which we are privileged to play a part.

The journey awaits, ever ancient and ever new. The word *adventure* has its roots in the Latin word *adventurus*, meaning "about to happen" or "about to arrive," which itself derives from *advenire*, "to come to." This etymology reflects the essence of embarking on a quest: It is an encounter with the unknown, a journey toward something that lies just beyond the horizon of our current understanding. To adventure is to embrace the unfolding of events that are yet to come, to step into the uncertainty with a heart open to whatever may arise, to be open to the mysteries of the transformative process. The call to adventure sounds anew in each moment. How will you answer?

Remember, courage is not the absence of fear. It is the alchemical art of transmuting the lead of fear into the gold of faith. Carry your fear with you as you walk the path, for it is through the crucible of experience that lead becomes gold. The treasure you seek isn't something external—it is the light you've carried within all along.

We are not waiting for gods to return from distant stars because they are already here. The gods never left. The true Anunnaki revelation is not that gods came from space, but that human consciousness can access otherworldly intelligence. The shamanic survivors we remember as the Anunnaki understood that consciousness itself is the ultimate technology, a living bridge to intelligences that exist beyond matter. They discovered that this technology of mind, rather than nuts-and-bolts spacecraft, is humanity's true cosmic inheritance. The Anunnaki were our ancestors on the path of awakening, showing us what we were always meant to become.

BIBLIOGRAPHY

Allegro, John M. 1970. *The Sacred Mushroom and the Cross: A Study of the Nature and Origins of Christianity Within the Fertility Cults of the Ancient Near East.* Hodder and Stoughton.

Antolín, Ferran. 2016. "Local, Intensive and Diverse? Early Farmers and Plant Economy in the North-East of the Iberian Peninsula (5500–2300 cal BC)." PhD diss., Universitat Autònoma de Barcelona.

Bakels, Corrie. 2007. "Nature or Culture? Cereal Crops Raised by Neolithic Farmers on Dutch Loess Soils." In *The Origins and Spread of Domestic Plants in Southwest Asia and Europe*, edited by Sue Colledge and James Conolly, 343–55. Left Coast Press.

Barber, Elizabeth Wayland. 1999. *The Mummies of Ürümchi.* W.W. Norton and Company.

Barton, George Aaron. 1918. *Miscellaneous Babylonian Inscriptions.* Kessinger Publishing.

Black, Jeremy, and Anthony Green. 1992. *Gods, Demons and Symbols of Ancient Mesopotamia: An Illustrated Dictionary.* University of Texas Press.

Boekhoven, J. G. 2011. *Ritualizing the Transcendent: Modern Magic in World Religion.* Amsterdam University Press.

Bogaard, Amy, et al. 2013. "Crop Manuring and Intensive Land Management by Europe's First Farmers." *Proceedings of the National Academy of Sciences* 110, no. 31: 12589–94.

Bostrom, Nick. 2005. "A History of Transhumanist Thought." *Journal of Evolution and Technology* 14, no. 1: 1–25.

Bottéro, Jean. 1992. *Mesopotamia: Writing, Reasoning, and the Gods.* University of Chicago Press.

Campbell, Joseph. 1949. *The Hero with a Thousand Faces.* Pantheon Books.

Carhart-Harris, Robin L., David Erritzoe, Tim Williams, et al. 2012. "Neural Correlates of the Psychedelic State as Determined by fMRI Studies with Psilocybin." *Proceedings of the National Academy of Sciences* 109, no. 6: 2138–43. *https://doi.org/10.1073/pnas.1119598109.*

Casanova, Michèle. *Le lapis-lazuli dans l'Orient ancien: Production et circulation du néolithique au IIe millénaire av.* J.-C. Éditions du Comité des Travaux Historiques et Scientifiques, 1991.

Chovanec, Zuzana, Soultana Maria Valamoti, Ganna Nikolova, and Petar Zidarov. 2015. "The Importance of Wild and Cultivated Plants as Potential Opium Sources in South East Europe and West Asia During Prehistory." *Archaeologica Bulgarica* 19, no. 3: 1–20.

CIA. 2003. "Analysis and Assessment of Gateway Process." Declassified document. *https://www.cia.gov/readingroom/docs/CIA-RDP96-00788R001700210016-5.pdf.*

Civil, Miguel. 1966. "Notes on Sumerian Lexicography, I." *Journal of Cuneiform Studies* 20: 119–24.

Collins, Andrew. 2024. *Karahan Tepe: Civilization of the Anunnaki and the Cosmic Origins of the Serpent of Eden.* Bear and Company.

Collon, Dominique. 2008. *The Queen of the Night: Exhibited with a Catalogue of Ancient Near Eastern Art.* British Museum Press.

Conybeare, F. C., trans. 1898. "The Testament of Solomon." *Jewish Quarterly Review.*

Cory, Isaac Preston. 1828. *The Ancient Fragments.* London: William Pickering.

Curtis, Adam, dir. 2002. *The Century of the Self.* Documentary. BBC.

Dalley, Stephanie. 2000. *Myths from Mesopotamia: Creation, the Flood, Gilgamesh, and Others.* Oxford University Press.

Durkheim, Émile. 2001. *The Elementary Forms of Religious Life.* Translated by Carol Cosman. Oxford University Press.

Electronic Text Corpus of Sumerian Literature (ETCLS). University of Oxford, Faculty of Oriental Studies. n.d. Accessed June 16, 2025. *etcsl.orinst.ox.ac.uk/.*

Eliade, Mircea. 1964. *Shamanism: Archaic Techniques of Ecstasy.* Princeton University Press.

Emboden, William A. 1981. "Transcultural Use of Narcotic Water Lilies in Ancient Egyptian and Maya Drug Ritual." *Journal of Ethnopharmacology* 3, no. 1: 39–83.

Everett, Hugh. 1957. "'Relative State' Formulation of Quantum Mechanics." *Reviews of Modern Physics* 29, no. 3 (July): 454–62. *https://doi.org/10.1103/RevModPhys.29.454*.

Filoramo, Giovanni. 1990. *A History of Gnosticism*. Basil Blackwell.

Finkelstein, J. J. 1966. "The Genealogy of the Hammurapi Dynasty." *Journal of Cuneiform Studies* 20, no. 3/4: 95–118.

Firestone, R. B., et al. 2007. "Evidence for an Extraterrestrial Impact 12,900 Years Ago That Contributed to the Megafaunal Extinctions and the Younger Dryas Cooling." *Proceedings of the National Academy of Sciences* 104, no. 41: 16016–21.

Foreign Office (FO) Records. Various documents. FO 371/3410, FO 371/16923, FO 371/18946, FO 371/23202, FO 371/23211, FO 371/23212, FO 371/37330, FO 372/873, FO 624/1, FO 624/20, FO 813/1. The National Archives, Kew, United Kingdom.

Frahm, Eckart. 2013. "Rising Prices in Ur-III Times: A New Text." *Journal of Near Eastern Studies* 72, no. 1: 1–12.

Frankl, Viktor E. 1946. *Man's Search for Meaning*. Beacon Press.

Furst, Peter T. 1972. *Flesh of the Gods: The Ritual Use of Hallucinogens*. Praeger.

Furst, Peter T. 1976. *Hallucinogens and Culture*. Chandler and Sharp.

Gardner, Laurence. 1996. *Bloodline of the Holy Grail: The Hidden Lineage of Jesus Revealed*. Element.

Gokhman, David, Malka Nissim-Rafina, Lily Agranat-Tamir, et al. 2020. "Differential DNA Methylation of Vocal and Facial Anatomy Genes in Modern Humans." *Nature Communications* 11, no. 1189 . *https://doi.org/10.1038/s41467-020-15020-6*.

Griffiths, R. R., W. A. Richards, U. McCann, et al. 2006. "Psilocybin Can Occasion Mystical-Type Experiences Having Substantial and Sustained Personal Meaning and Spiritual Significance." *Psychopharmacology* 187, no. 3: 268–83.

Grof, Stanislav. 1985. *Beyond the Brain: Birth, Death, and Transcendence in Psychotherapy*. State University of New York Press.

Hamilton, Edith. 1942. *Mythology*. Little, Brown and Company.

Hancock, Graham. 1995. *Fingerprints of the Gods: The Evidence of Earth's Lost Civilization*. Crown Publishers.

Hanegraaff, Wouter J. 1996. *New Age Religion and Western Culture: Esotericism in the Mirror of Secular Thought*. Brill.

Harner, Michael. 1990. *The Way of the Shaman*. Harper and Row.

Heiser, Michael S. n.d. "The Myth of a Sumerian 12th Planet: 'Nibiru' According to the Cuneiform Sources." SitchinIsWrong.com. Accessed July 28, 2025. *sitchiniswrong.com.*

Hopkins, Marilyn, and Tim Wallace-Murphy. 2000. *Rex Deus: The True Mystery of Rennes-le-Château and the Dynasty of Jesus.*

Hussein, Muzahim Mahmoud. 2016. *Nimrud: The Queens' Tombs*. Translated and edited by Mark Altaweel; notes by McGuire Gibson. Iraqi State Board of Antiquities and Chicago: Oriental Institute.

Jacobsen, Thorkild. 1939. *The Sumerian King List*. University of Chicago Press.

Jaynes, Julian. 1976. *The Origin of Consciousness in the Breakdown of the Bicameral Mind*. Houghton Mifflin Company.

Jesus, Ana, et al. 2021. "Geometric Morphometrics as a Tool to Identify Papaver Somniferum L. Subspecies and Varieties." *Scientific Reports* 11, no. 1: 1–13.

Jung, Carl G. 1960. *The Structure and Dynamics of the Psyche*. Pantheon Books.

Kantor, Helene J. 1947. "The Aegean and the Orient in the Second Millennium B.C." *American Journal of Archaeology* 51, no. 1 (January–March): 1–103.

Kasak, Enn, and Raul Veede. 2001. "Understanding Planets in Ancient Mesopotamia." *Folklore* 16. *https://doi.org/10.7592/FEJF2001.16.planets.*

Kassian, Alexei. 2014. "Lexical Matches Between Sumerian and Hurro-Urartian: Possible Historical Scenarios." *Cuneiform Digital Library Journal* no. 4.

Kellens, Jean.1989. *Essays on Zarathustra and Zoroastrianism*. Mazda Publishers.

Kindy, David. 2022. "U.S. Returns 4,000-Year-Old Cuneiform Tablet and Prism to Iraq." *Smithsonian Magazine*, February 1. *www.smithsonianmag.com.*

Kislev, Mordechai E., Anat Hartmann, and Ehud Galili. 2004. "Archaeobotanical and Archaeoentomological Evidence from a Well at Atlit-Yam

Indicates Colder, More Humid Climate on the Israeli Coast during the PPNC Period." *Journal of Archaeological Science* 31, no. 9 (September): 1301–10.

Koestler, Arthur. 1976. *The Thirteenth Tribe: The Khazar Empire and Its Heritage.* Random House.

Kohl, Philip L. 2009. *The Making of Bronze Age Eurasia.* Cambridge University Press.

Kramer, Samuel Noah. 1963. *The Sumerians: Their History, Culture, and Character.* University of Chicago Press.

Kreuz, Angela, et al. 2005. "A Comparison of Early Neolithic Crop and Weed Assemblages from the Linearbandkeramik and the Bulgarian Neolithic Cultures: Differences and Similarities." *Vegetation History and Archaeobotany* 14, no. 4: 237–58.

Kripal, Jeffrey J. 2007. *Esalen: America and the Religion of No Religion.* University of Chicago Press.

Kurzweil, Ray. 2005. *The Singularity Is Near: When Humans Transcend Biology.* Viking.

Lamberg-Karlovsky, C. C. 2003. "Archaeological Investigations in the Sogan Valley, Southeast Iran." *Iran* 11: 147–53.

Lambert, W. G. 1984. "Studies in Marduk." *Bulletin of the School of Oriental and African Studies* 47: 1–9.

Lazar, Bob. 1989. "Bob Lazar on 'The Billy Goodman Happening,'" YouTube, posted by Historia Discordia, May 8, 2020. *youtube.com.*

Lenzi, Alan. 2008. *Secrecy and the Gods: Secret Knowledge in Ancient Mesopotamia and Biblical Israel.* Neo-Assyrian Text Corpus Project.

Levi, Eliphas. 1896. *Transcendental Magic: Its Doctrine and Ritual.* Translated by A. E. Waite. London: George Redway.

Luke, David. 2011. "Discarnate Entities and Dimethyltryptamine." *Journal of the Society for Psychical Research*, 75 no. 899 (January): 26–42.

Mair, Victor H. 2016. "Ancient Mummies of the Tarim Basin." *Expedition Magazine* 58, no. 2. *penn.museum.*

Majidzadeh, Yusef. 2003. "Jiroft: The Earliest Oriental Civilization." *Iranian Journal of Archaeology* 14: 1–7.

Maslow, Abraham H. 1968. *Toward a Psychology of Being.* Van Nostrand.

McKenna, Terence. 1992. *Food of the Gods: The Search for the Original Tree of Knowledge*. Bantam.

Merlin, Mark David. 1984. *On the Trail of the Ancient Opium Poppy*. Associated University Presses.

Merlin, Mark David. 2003. "Archaeological Evidence for the Tradition of Psychoactive Plant Use in the Old World." *Economic Botany* 57, no. 3: 295–323.

Mill, John Stuart. 1867. *Dissertations and Discussions: Political, Philosophical, and Historical*. London: Longmans, Green, Reader, and Dyer.

Mithen, Steven. 1996. *The Prehistory of the Mind: The Cognitive Origins of Art, Religion and Science*. Thames and Hudson.

Muscarella, Oscar White. 2003. "Archaeology, Artifacts, and Antiquities of the Ancient Near East: Sites, Cultures, and Proveniences." *Journal of Field Archaeology* 30, no. 3: 291–316.

Needham, Joseph. 1980. *Science and Civilisation in China, Vol. 3: Mathematics and the Sciences of the Heavens and the Earth*. Cambridge University Press.

Nietzsche, Friedrich. 2003. *Thus Spoke Zarathustra*. Translated by R. J. Hollingdale. Penguin.

Nietzsche, Friedrich. 1989. *Beyond Good and Evil*. Translated by Walter Kaufmann. Vintage.

O'Brien, Christian, and Barbara Joy O'Brien. 1997. *The Shining Ones: A Visitor's Guide to the Sumerian Gods*. Element Books.

Oers, Lotte. 2010. "A Round Peg in a Square Hole? The Sikkatu in Old Babylonian Susa." *Akkadica* 131: 1–42.

Orrelle, Estelle. 2022. "Identifying Iconographic Evidence for a Mushroom Cult in the Preliterate Southern Levant." *Time and Mind* 15, no. 4: 1–20. *https://doi.org/10.1080/1751696X.2022.2119096*.

Oshima, Takayoshi. 2014. *Babylonian Poems of Pious Sufferers*. Mohr Siebeck.

Pasulka, Paula. 2020. *The Unidentified: Mythical Monsters, Alien Encounters, and Our Obsession with the Unexplained*. Dutton.

Perrot, J., and Y. Majidzadeh. 2005. "The Art of Chlorite and Cultural Connections Between Jiroft and Mesopotamia." *Iranica Antiqua* 40: 33–52.

Peters, John P. 1908. "The Nippur Archive." *Journal of the American Oriental Society* 29.

Peters, John P. 1908. "Reply to Hilprecht's Answer." Unpublished manuscript. Princeton University Library.

Pinker, Steven. 1997. *How the Mind Works.* W.W. Norton and Company.

Pliny the Elder. 1855. *Natural History*. Translated by John Bostock and H. T. Riley. Taylor and Francis.

Plutarch. 1927. *Isis and Osiris.* Translated by Frank Cole Babbitt. Loeb Classical Library. Harvard University Press.

Pringle, Heather. 2006. *The Master Plan: Himmler's Scholars and the Holocaust.* Hyperion.

Reich, David, et al. 2010. "Genetic History of an Archaic Hominin Group from Denisova Cave in Siberia." *Nature* 468, no. 7327: 1053–60.

Reich, David. 2018. *Who We Are and How We Got Here: Ancient DNA and the New Science of the Human Past.* Pantheon.

Reiner, Erica. 1961. "The Etiological Myth of the 'Seven Sages.'" *Orientalia* 30, no. 1: 1–11.

Rogan, Joe. 2024. "The Joe Rogan Experience #2028—Jeremy Corbell & George Knapp." YouTube posted by PowerfulJRE, June 27. *youtube.com.*

Rothfield, Lawrence. 2009. *The Rape of Mesopotamia: Behind the Looting of the Iraq Museum.* University of Chicago Press.

Rössner, Corinna, et al. 2018. "Tracking the Introduction of Opium Poppy into Ancient Anatolia Through Archaeobotanical Evidence." *Vegetation History and Archaeobotany* 27, no. 2: 319–30.

Rottoli, Mauro, and Andrea Pessina. 2007. "Neolithic Agriculture in Italy: An Update of Archaeobotanical Data with Particular Emphasis on Northern Settlements." In *The Origins and Spread of Domestic Plants in Southwest Asia and Europe.* Edited by Sue Colledge and James Conolly, 140–53. Left Coast Press.

Ruck, Carl A. P., Jeremy Bigwood, Danny Staples, Jonathan Ott, and R. Gordon Wasson. 1979. "Entheogens." *Journal of Psychedelic Drugs* 11, no. 1–2: 145–46.

Ruck, Carl A. P., Blaise Daniel Staples, Clark Heinrich, Mark Hoffman, and José Alfredo González Celdrán. *The Hidden World: Survival of Pagan Shamanic Themes in European Fairytales.* Oakville, CT: Book Tree, 2001.

Rudgley, Richard. 1999. *The Lost Civilizations of the Stone Age.* Free Press.

Salavert, Aurélie, et al. 2020. "The Opium Poppy in Europe: Exploring Its Origin and Dispersal During the Neolithic." *Antiquity* 94, no. 376: 789–805.

Scholem, Gershom. 1946. *Major Trends in Jewish Mysticism.* Schocken Books.

Schultes, Richard Evans, and Albert Hofmann. 1979. *Plants of the Gods: Origins of Hallucinogenic Use.* McGraw-Hill.

Sieckmeyer, K. 2024. "Tonpilz—Königsinschrift zur falschen Zeit am falschen Ort." (Tonpilz—Royal Inscription at the Wrong Time in the Wrong Place). In *Uruk-Warka-Sammlung des Deutschen Archäologischen Instituts.* Uruk-Warka Collection, University of Heidelberg, n.d. Accessed July 29, 2024. *uni-heidelberg.de.*

Sitchin, Zecharia. 1976. *The 12th Planet.* Harper, 1976.

Sommerfeld, Walter (1982). *Der Aufstieg Marduks: Die Stellung Marduks in der babylonischen Religion des zweiten Jahrtausends v. Chr.* Butzon and Bercker.

Stone-Miller, Rebecca. 2002. *Art of the Andes: From Chavín to Inca.* Thames and Hudson.

Strassman, Rick. 2001. *DMT: The Spirit Molecule.* Park Street Press.

Strieber, Whitley. 2011. Interview by Tim Weisberg. *Spooky Southcoast.* Episode no. 254, aired May 28. Audio, 1:37:00. *spookysouthcoast.com.*

Terry, Charles E. and Mildred Pellens. 1928. *The Opium Problem.* Patterson Smith.

Thomas, Chan. 1963. *The Adam and Eve Story.* Bengal Tiger Press.

Thompson, R. Campbell. 1900. *The Reports of the Magicians and Astrologers of Nineveh and Babylon in the British Museum.* London: Luzac and Co.

Torijano, Pablo A. 2002. *Solomon the Esoteric King: From King to Magus, Development of a Tradition.* Brill.

Unterländer, Martina, et al. 2017. "Ancestry and Demography and Descendants of Iron Age Nomads of the Eurasian Steppe." *Nature Communications* 8: 14615.

van Buren, Elizabeth Douglas. 1950. "The Ṣalmê in Mesopotamian Art and Religion." *Orientalia* 19: 97–134.

Wang, Chuan-Chao, et al. 2019. "Ancient Human Genome-Wide Data from a 3000-Year Interval in the Caucasus Corresponds with Eco-Geographic Regions." *Nature Communications* 10, no. 1: 590.

Wasson, R. Gordon, Albert Hofmann, and Carl A. P. Ruck. 1978. *The Road to Eleusis: Unveiling the Secret of the Mysteries*. Harcourt Brace Jovanovich.

Wiener, Norbert. 1948. *Cybernetics: Or Control and Communication in the Animal and the Machine*. MIT Press.

Wiggermann, Frans A. M. 1992. *Mesopotamian Protective Spirits: The Ritual Texts*. Cuneiform Monographs 1. Styx Publications.

Wilkinson, Richard H. 2003. *The Complete Gods and Goddesses of Ancient Egypt*. Thames and Hudson.

Wrangham, Richard. 2009. *Catching Fire: How Cooking Made Us Human*. Basic Books.

Zaehner, R. C. 1961. *The Dawn and Twilight of Zoroastrianism*. Weidenfeld and Nicolson.

Zhang, Fan, et al. 2021."The Genomic Origins of the Bronze Age Tarim Basin Mummies." *Nature* 599, no. 7884: 256–61.

Zohary, Daniel, Maria Hopf, and Ehud Weiss. 2012. *Domestication of Plants in the Old World: The Origin and Spread of Domesticated Plants in Southwest Asia, Europe, and the Mediterranean Basin*. 4th ed. Oxford University Press.

ABOUT THE AUTHOR

Dr. Heather Lynn is a historian, adjunct professor, museum Director, and author of *The Anunnaki Connection*, *Evil Archaeology*, and *Baphomet Revealed*. Heather holds degrees in archaeology, information technology, and history, as well as a doctorate in education from the University of New England. She has spent decades uncovering the hidden connections between ancient mystery schools and modern technology, and tracked how the same consciousness-altering techniques used by the ancients are now being weaponized in AI and Big Tech. As a consulting expert for museums and media, she regularly appears on History's *Ancient Aliens*, where she contributes insights on everything from occult symbolism to archaeological suppression. She also hosts *The Midnight Academy* podcast, available on YouTube and all major platforms, where she explores the deeper mysteries of consciousness, culture, and the hidden past.

Beyond her research and teaching, Heather plays French horn in a regional symphony whose performances support arts and cultural education for underserved communities. She finds grounding in classical and liturgical music, meditation, hiking, tennis, flower gardening, and a good cup of tea.

www.drheatherlynn.com